# The Meat-Free Kitchen

Inspiring | Educating | Creating | Entertaining

Brimming with creative inspiration, how-to projects, and useful information to enrich your everyday life, Quarto Knows is a favorite destination for those pursuing their interests and passions. Visit our site and dig deeper with our books into your area of interest: Quarto Creates, Quarto Cooks, Quarto Homes, Quarto Lives, Quarto Drives, Quarto Explores, Quarto Gifts, or Quarto Kids.

The content in this book previously appeared in *The Best Veggie Burgers on the Planet, Revised and Updated*, by Joni Marie Newman (Fair Winds Press 2019); *Buddha Bowls*, by Kelli Foster (The Harvard Common Press 2018); and *The Meatless Monday Family Cookbook*, by Jenn Sebestyen (Fair Winds Press 2019).

Cover and Page Design: Maggie Cote

Photography: Alison Bickel Photography, Maria Siriano, and Celine Steen

# The Meat-Free Kitchen

Super Healthy and Incredibly Delicious
Vegetarian Meals for All Day, Every Day

Jenn Sebestyen, Kelli Foster, and Joni Marie Newman

FAIR WINDS

# CONTENTS

# Introduction

Welcome!

Let's get this out of the way, first thing: This book is for everyone. It's for those who want to incorporate more vegetables in their diet. It's for those who want to make sure their family gets their daily dose of fruits and veggies. It's for those who want to dabble in eating meatless once a week or even just once a month. It's for those who want to stop eating meat altogether. It's for those with dairy intolerance or allergies who need some yummy dairy-free options. It's for those who are already rocking a plant-based diet and are looking for more delicious variety. It's for everyone who loves good food!

Eating a plant-based diet can be healthy, satisfying, and totally delicious. And you don't have to be a talented chef to eat this way. The nearly 300 recipes in this book are for all skill levels in the kitchen. Most of the recipes are easy and fuss-free; a few are more involved, but they're oh-so-worth-it.

## START YOUR MEATLESS LIFE TODAY

Reducing your meat intake and incorporating more vegetables and fruits into your daily routine—starting today—is not only easier and more convenient than you think, but also it's better for you and better for the planet. Whether you decide to do this for one day, one week, one month, or forever after is a choice you need to make for yourself. Even one meal per week is a great start if you can't commit to a whole day.

Whether you want to go meatless for health reasons, environmental causes, animal welfare, or economic concerns, this book will give you some great tips about how to get started and how to stock your pantry so a healthy meatless meal is always in reach.

If you are used to eating meat with nearly every meal, here are two easy ways to ditch it:

**#1 Start with flavors and meals you're familiar with and just leave out the meat.**

For example: Spaghetti and meatballs. Simply leave out the meatballs. Serve the spaghetti with marinara sauce, garlic bread, and an easy side salad. Or go one step further and add lentils to the sauce instead of meat. Don't expect these meals to have the exact same taste and texture that you're used to. Just appreciate them as the delicious meals they are.

**#2 Try new flavors and dishes that you've never had.**

If you have no preconceived notions of how something should taste, you may be more willing to forget the fact that there is no meat on your plate.

Whichever option you choose, just start. It really is that easy. Find a recipe you think sounds delicious, buy the ingredients you need, and enjoy it. Don't worry about having a fully stocked pantry and fridge. Take it one day or one meal at a time. There is nothing wrong with going at your own pace.

That being said, it's helpful to know about the ingredients you're likely to use most often for your meatless meals.

## MEATLESS PANTRY ESSENTIALS

A well-stocked kitchen is essential to getting meals, regardless of whether they're plant-based, on the table quickly and without frustration. Many of these items may be familiar to you, while a few others may be new to you. For the most part, they are easy to find at most grocery stores, and you'll get good use out of them.

Don't feel that you must have all these items stocked all at once. Over time, you'll build up your pantry, spices, and nonperishables. As you become comfortable cooking with these ingredients, you'll find that many can be interchanged or substituted to suit your family's tastes. If you have a few items on hand from each category, you'll be able to make delicious, nutritious meals.

### Legumes

Legumes are full of healthy plant-based protein, and they're low in fat. They're inexpensive and incredibly versatile. While bags of dried beans and lentils are inexpensive, you can't deny the convenience of canned. And don't forget about frozen shelled edamame (soybeans).

### Grains

Full of fiber and protein, whole grains keep us feeling satiated. They bring loads of different textures, and there are quite a few gluten-free options. They're just as great for breakfast as they are for dinner. A few grains that cook up in less than 20 minutes include quick-cook brown rice (the nutrient difference between quick-cook and regular brown rice is minimal), jasmine rice, quinoa, and oats.

For the most part, the grains in this book are interchangeable. If you're making a bowl that calls for quinoa, but you'd rather use farro, go right ahead. (Stick to the grain called for in burger recipes, unless noted, to maintain optimal consistency.)

As for flour, most gluten-free blends can stand in for all-purpose flour. You'll note some recipes call for vital wheat gluten flour. Gluten is the natural protein portion removed from whole wheat. It is important to note that vital wheat gluten flour is completely different from high gluten flour. The two are not interchangeable and will not perform similarly in recipes.

In addition to traditional grains and noodles, several Buddha bowl recipes in this book use gluten-free grain alternatives, like riced cauliflower and broccoli, as well as zucchini, sweet potato, and beet noodles. You're certainly not going to confuse vegetable rices and noodles for the real thing, but sometimes you just want an extra serving of vegetables. And it's easy (and less expensive) to make many of them at home; there are directions in the recipes that call for them.

### Pasta

Pasta can be made from grains, beans, or even vegetables and it comes in a variety of shapes and sizes to suit almost any dish. There are plenty of gluten-free varieties available today as well. And this much is true: add noodles to just about any dish and it just got a whole lot more kid-friendly.

### Nuts and Seeds

Raw nuts and seeds contain healthy fats and protein. They are great for snacking and adding crunch to meals. They can even be used to create creamy sauces. Nut and seed butters are wonderful on toast or crackers, and they can be stirred into sauces for depth of flavor. Look for nut butters that are just ground nuts and, maybe, salt.

### Dried Spices and Herbs

Welcome to the easiest and most affordable way to add flavor to your recipes. Fresh herbs are great to finish a dish, but it's the dried herbs and spices that you'll use the most. While dried herbs and spices won't spoil, you won't be getting their full flavor if you haven't replaced them in a few years. Although each recipe lists specific amounts for every ingredient, taste before serving and adjust the seasoning to your liking. Most spices used in this book are ones you probably grew up with, with some additions like garam masala, turmeric, and black salt.

### Oils

Due to its high fat content, oil brings flavor, richness, and moisture to a dish. For high-heat cooking, panfrying, or roasting, try avocado oil, coconut oil (also in spray), and peanut oil. Choose regular olive oil for sautéing and extra-virgin for sauces and dressings. And Asian-inspired dishes get a great flavor boost by finishing with sesame oil. If you want to go oil-free, to sauté, try using ¼ cup (60 ml) of water or broth and add more as needed to prevent sticking.

### Condiments and Flavorings

These are the ingredients that are going to take your dishes from good to great. Sometimes just a spoonful or two is all you need. You may not always detect them in the finished dish, but they will bring depth of flavor and add that extra something. Some you're already familiar with, such as all varieties of vinegar, sriracha and other hot sauces, and lemon/lime juice. But there are others that might be new to you:

- **Coconut Aminos (gluten-free and soy-free), Tamari (gluten-free), and Soy Sauce:** These are all basically interchangeable.

- **Liquid Smoke:** This flavoring is stocked near the marinades in most markets. It's actually made by condensing smoke into liquid form. A little goes a long way in giving a smoky flavor to many foods.

- **Mellow White Miso Paste:** Miso is fermented soybean paste. Generally, the soybeans are combined with grains, such as rice or barley. If you are gluten-free, you will need to check the label to see which kind of grains are used. It will keep in the fridge almost indefinitely, so no worries about it going bad before you have a chance to use it.

- **Nutritional Yeast:** This is a deactivated yeast. Although it's technically made from the same type of yeast, it is not the same as brewer's yeast or baker's yeast. Most often you'll find fortified nutritional yeast, which is a complete protein and contains vitamins and minerals. Most brands contain vitamin $B_{12}$, which is sometimes hard to get enough of on a plant-based diet. The taste is savory and a little nutty—some say cheesy.

- **Seaweed, such as hijiki, dulse, and nori:** Dried, edible seaweeds add a fishy flavor to foods without using fish.

- **Tahini:** Tahini is sesame seed paste with a texture like peanut butter; it has a savory, slightly nutty taste that can be a bit bitter but is easily balanced with other ingredients, such as vinegar and pure maple syrup.

- **Worcestershire Sauce:** While you might know that Worcestershire sauce has an unmistakable savory, yet sweet and tangy, taste, look for a brand that says vegan on the label to avoid anchovies.

## Meat Substitutes

This book uses a variety of meat substitutes, some that you buy and some that you make:

- **Jackfruit:** This tropical fruit can grow as big as 120 pounds (54 kg)! The ripe fruit is sweet and tastes like a cross between a banana and a pineapple. This book calls for unripened "Young Green" jackfruit in cans. Make sure to pick up cans packed in water or brine, and not syrup. When cooked, it mimics shredded meats and has very little flavor on its own.

- **Tempeh:** Tempeh is made from fermented soybeans pressed into a cake. Bitter to some, this whole-bean soy treat is a very versatile protein. Simmering tempeh in water or vegetable broth for about 20 minutes prior to using in recipes mellows the flavor.

- **Tofu:** There are a few different types and textures out there. Soft silken tofu is best used for sauces and blended desserts, while it's best to use super firm or extra firm for other recipes, and press before using. To press tofu, simply lay drained tofu on a clean folded kitchen towel. Place another clean towel on top and then top with a heavy skillet or book to press excess moisture out of the tofu.

- **TVP (Textured Vegetable Protein):** This high-protein, low-fat ingredient is made from defatted soybeans. The oil is extruded from the beans, leaving behind a malleable mass that can be formed into shapes and dehydrated. This makes it shelf-stable and the perfect meat substitute to have on hand in your pantry. It's available in many forms, like chunks, granules, and strips. The recipes in this book call for granules. Since it's dried, TVP does need to be reconstituted. Here are some tips:

    - When microwaving, use plastic wrap to tightly cover your bowl or container. (If that freaks you out, bring liquid to a boil, pour it over the TVP granules, cover tightly, and let stand for 10 minutes.)

    - Use 1 cup (235 ml) of liquid per 1 cup (96 g) of TVP when reconstituting, unless otherwise noted.

    - Use vegetable broth instead of water for more flavorful TVP.

    - You can reconstitute a large batch of TVP all at once, and then store in an airtight container in the fridge. It should keep for up to a week.

## Other Pantry Staples

Other ingredients that are useful to keep stocked in your pantry include canned tomato products, full-fat and lite coconut milks (canned), mayo (egg-free if you wish), pure maple syrup, roasted red peppers, salsa (traditional tomato-based and salsa verde), tortillas (flour, corn, or other gluten-free options). Among nondairy milks, soymilk, almond milk, or coconut milk seems to yield the best results when cooking, but use the milk you're most comfortable with (even if that's dairy milk!).

# A NOTE ABOUT THE RECIPES

Throughout this book, you will see suggestions for omitting soy or gluten. Many of the recipes are already gluten-free. For most others, there are notes on how to make them gluten-free. *But always check labels*. If you have food allergies or are on a restricted diet, double-check ingredients, especially vinegars, flavor extracts, soy sauces, and other store-bought items.

You will also notice the use of dairy products such as *sour cream, milk, yogurt, butter, cheese,* and so on. If you are vegan or otherwise avoiding dairy, opt for the vegan versions of these items. (In some cases, you'll be able to make your own.)

There's something for everyone in these pages. The recipes span the globe, from Latin America to northern Africa to Southeast Asia—and countless ports in between. Many recipes have families in mind and are suitable for tiny taste buds. Whether you're looking for breakfast (breakfast *burgers*, anyone?), beautiful Buddha bowls, hearty sandwiches, filling casseroles, or a tasty side dish, this book has you covered. Now let's get cooking!

*1*

# YUMMY BREAKFASTS

Just as you might sometimes eat dinner leftovers for breakfast, you might also occasionally bring out the breakfast vibes for dinner. This chapter is packed with options that will fit both bills. There's your traditional breakfast fare of oats and the like, loads of beautiful wholesome bowls, and savory burgers that will hit the spot no matter what time of day.

# Peanut Butter Pancakes with Maple–Peanut Butter Syrup

If you love peanut butter, this recipe is for you. There's peanut butter in the pancakes and peanut butter in the syrup. It's sweet and indulgent and oh-so-good.

**FOR PEANUT BUTTER PANCAKES:**
1½ cups (180 g) spelt flour or (188 g) all-purpose flour
2 teaspoons baking powder
½ teaspoon salt
¼ teaspoon ground cinnamon (optional)
½ cup (130 g) organic natural peanut butter
1¾ cups (410 ml) unsweetened plain almond milk or milk of choice
3 tablespoons (60 g) pure maple syrup
1 teaspoon vanilla extract
Cooking spray

**FOR MAPLE–PEANUT BUTTER SYRUP:**
¼ cup (65 g) organic natural peanut butter
2 tablespoons (40 g) pure maple syrup
4–6 tablespoons (60–90 ml) unsweetened plain almond milk or milk of choice
¼ teaspoon vanilla extract (optional)
Dash of cinnamon (optional)

**TOPPINGS (OPTIONAL):**
Banana slices
Chocolate chips
Chopped raw peanuts

**Yield: 4 to 6 servings**

**For the Peanut Butter Pancakes:** In a large mixing bowl, whisk together the flour, baking powder, salt, and cinnamon, if using.

In a large measuring cup, whisk together the peanut butter, almond milk, maple syrup, and vanilla.

Pour the wet ingredients into the dry ingredients and stir until just combined. Set aside for about 10 minutes to let the batter thicken up.

Lightly spray a nonstick skillet with cooking spray and heat over medium heat. Once hot, pour ¼ cup (60 ml) of batter for each pancake. Do not crowd the pan; do two at a time. You might be able to fit three if you have a large pan.

Cook each pancake for about 3 to 5 minutes. It's ready to flip when the edges start turning lightly brown and bubbles begin to pop on top of the pancake. Gently flip and cook for another 3 to 5 minutes. Transfer to a plate and continue until all the batter has been used. You might need to add more cooking spray before adding each new batch to the pan. You also may need to adjust the heat as you go. The pan will get hotter the longer you use it, so just watch your pancakes and turn down the heat a bit if necessary.

**For the Maple–Peanut Butter Syrup:** Whisk together all the ingredients listed. Try not to drink it before your pancakes are ready—it's so darn good!

Serve the Peanut Butter Pancakes with any of the optional toppings, if desired, and a good drizzle of the Maple–Peanut Butter Syrup.

# The Best Oatmeal Bowl

This recipe is really more about the method and a few basic ingredients. The toppings are what's going to make it your own. You can switch them up to make a different version every time, so you never get bored. But stick with this basic method and you will fall in love with oatmeal.

Mash the bananas with a fork until they resemble a purée.

Add the water to a pot on the stove. Whisk in the banana until well incorporated.

Add the oats to the cold water and then turn on the stove to medium-high. As soon as the oatmeal comes to a simmer, add the peanut butter and cinnamon, if using, turn down the heat to low, and cook until the desired consistency, stirring occasionally. This generally takes less than 10 minutes.

Spoon into individual bowls. Top with (or stir in) your ingredients of choice. Some of our favorite combos are: peanut butter, diced apple, cinnamon, and hemp seeds; almond butter, frozen blueberries, a dash of powdered ginger, and a drizzle of pure maple syrup; and peanut butter, fresh sliced banana, dairy-free chocolate chips, and shredded coconut.

**FOR OATMEAL:**

2 ripe bananas, smashed well (Use just one if you are not a banana lover.)

3¼ cups (760 g) cold water

2 cups (160 g) old-fashioned rolled oats

2 heaping tablespoons (about 40 g) peanut butter or almond butter

½ teaspoon ground cinnamon (optional)

**TOPPINGS:**

Extra dollop of nut butter

Sprinkle of chopped nuts or seeds

Fresh fruit

Dried fruit

Spices such as ground cinnamon, nutmeg, or ginger

Chocolate chips

Granola

Pure maple syrup

**Yield: 4 servings**

**Note:** For a gluten-free version, make sure to choose certified gluten-free oats. For a nut-free version, use sunflower seed butter instead of nut butter.

# Oatmeal Cookie Granola Parfait

Here's a breakfast that tastes like dessert. Throw it in a container and take it on-the-go. Pack it in a lunch box. Or layer it up with yogurt and fruit and make a pretty parfait.

**FOR OATMEAL COOKIE GRANOLA (MAKES ABOUT 2 CUPS [220 G]):**

1½ cups (120 g) old-fashioned rolled oats

1 cup (30 g) crisp brown rice cereal

½ cup (160 g) pure maple syrup

1 teaspoon vanilla extract

1½ teaspoons ground cinnamon

¼ teaspoon salt

¼ cup (35 g) raisins, (60 g) chocolate chips, or both (optional)

**FOR PARFAIT:**

2 cups (460 g) plain or flavored yogurt

2 cups (weight will vary) fruit (blueberries, sliced strawberries, diced apple, etc.)

**Yield: 4 servings**

**For the Oatmeal Cookie Granola:** Preheat the oven to 300°F (150°C, or gas mark 2). Line a rimmed baking sheet with parchment paper and set aside.

Combine the oats and crisp brown rice cereal in a mixing bowl.

In a small bowl or cup, whisk together the maple syrup, vanilla, cinnamon, and salt.

Pour the wet ingredients over the dry ingredients while stirring to incorporate. Mix well to ensure all the dry ingredients are coated.

Spread out onto the prepared baking sheet into one compact even layer. Pat it down, but don't spread it out too much; you don't want gaps in between.

Bake for 30 minutes. Turn your pan around in the oven at the 20-minute mark to ensure even cooking because our oven does have some hot spots. DO NOT STIR during the cooking time. Let it cool on the pan for about 10 minutes and then break into clumps. Let the granola continue to cool completely.

Stir in the raisins or chocolate chips, or both, if using.

**To assemble the parfaits:** Dollop some yogurt in the bottom of a glass or small bowl. Top with a sprinkle of granola and some fruit. Repeat 2 or 3 times for each parfait. If preparing in advance, put all the granola on top or in a separate container and mix when ready to serve.

# Banana Walnut Baked Oatmeal

You should make this baked oatmeal just for the kitchen smells alone—rich bananas, sweet cinnamon and maple syrup, and nutty oats and walnuts. It's best served warm with fresh sliced bananas and an extra drizzle of syrup.

Preheat the oven to 350°F (180°C, or gas mark 4). Line an 8- × 8-inch (20 × 20 cm) baking dish with parchment paper or spray it lightly with cooking spray. Set aside.

In a large mixing bowl, stir together the oats, flaxseed meal, baking powder, cinnamon, salt, and walnuts.

In a small mixing bowl, whisk together the banana, maple syrup, almond milk, and vanilla.

Pour the wet ingredients into the dry ingredients. Stir well to combine, scraping down the sides of the bowl as necessary to ensure everything is coated.

Pour the mixture in the prepared baking dish. Bake for 25 to 30 minutes until set.

Let cool for 10 minutes before cutting and serving.

Top with fresh sliced banana, a sprinkle of hemp seeds, and an extra drizzle of pure maple syrup, if desired.

3 cups (240 g) old-fashioned rolled oats
2 tablespoons (14 g) flaxseed meal (ground flaxseeds)
1½ teaspoons baking powder
1 teaspoon ground cinnamon
½ teaspoon salt
½ cup (50 g) raw walnuts, chopped
1 ripe banana, mashed
½ cup (160 g) pure maple syrup, plus more for serving
1 cup (235 ml) unsweetened plain almond milk or milk of choice
½ teaspoon vanilla extract
Fresh banana slices, for topping
Hemp seeds, for topping

**Yield: 6 servings**

**Note:** For a nut-free version, leave out the walnuts. For extra indulgence, add ½ cup (87 g) of chocolate chips.

# Chickpea Scramble Breakfast Burrito

Protein-packed chickpeas mingle with Tex-Mex spices and superfood spinach all cozy-like in a big ol' burrito. This chickpea scramble is just as good on its own as it is stuffed into a tortilla. Try it both ways!

1 tablespoon (15 ml) olive oil

½ yellow onion, diced

½ red bell pepper, seeded and diced

2 cloves garlic, minced

1 teaspoon chili powder, or more to taste

½ teaspoon ground cumin

½ teaspoon ground turmeric

½ teaspoon salt, or to taste

¼ teaspoon black pepper, or to taste

1 can (15 ounces, or 425 g) chickpeas, drained and rinsed (or 1½ cups [246 g] cooked chickpeas)

Juice of ½ lemon

2 tablespoons (8 g) nutritional yeast (optional)

2 cups (60 g) fresh spinach, well chopped

4 large burrito-size tortillas

½ cup (130 g) salsa

1 avocado, peel and pit removed, sliced

**Yield: 4 servings**

**Note:** You may use gluten-free tortillas if desired but note that corn tortillas don't bend well and may break.

Heat the olive oil over medium heat in a large skillet. Add the onion and sauté for 5 to 6 minutes until soft and translucent. Add the bell pepper and garlic and sauté for 3 to 4 minutes until starting to soften.

Add the chili powder, cumin, turmeric, salt, and pepper. Sauté for 1 to 2 minutes until fragrant.

Add the chickpeas. Using a potato masher or a fork, mash about half of the chickpeas. Add the lemon juice and nutritional yeast, if using. Simmer for 5 to 10 minutes until some of the liquid has absorbed and the mixture is thick. Add the spinach and stir to combine. Sauté for 1 to 2 minutes to slightly wilt the spinach.

Wrap the tortillas in a just-damp paper towel and heat in the microwave for 20 to 30 seconds at a time until warm. Lay one tortilla flat and add one-quarter of the chickpea scramble on one end. On top of the scramble, add 2 tablespoons (33 g) of salsa and a few slices of avocado. Fold up the bottom half of the tortilla over the filling, then fold in both sides, and then starting from the bottom, tightly roll up the tortilla to form the burrito. Repeat with the remaining ingredients.

# Blackberry Millet Breakfast Bowls

If you have a thing for steel-cut oats, you should really give this millet bowl a try. Millet retains that firm, chewy texture similar to steel-cut oats, though it cooks in a fraction of the time. Go ahead and swap in raspberries, chopped strawberries, blueberries, or even a mixture. If you make the millet in advance, hold off on adding the yogurt and toppings until serving.

Combine the millet, milk, water, ½ cup (75 g) of the berries, ginger, and a pinch of salt in a medium saucepan. Bring to a boil, then reduce the heat to low, cover, and simmer until tender but not all the liquid has been absorbed, about 15 minutes. Stir occasionally and break up the berries with a spoon as they soften. Remove from the heat and steam with the lid on for 5 minutes. Stir in the honey and vanilla.

Meanwhile, whisk the lemon juice into the yogurt.

To serve, divide the millet among bowls. Top with the yogurt mixture, the remaining 1 cup (145 g) blackberries, walnuts, coconut, and a drizzle of honey.

1 cup (165 g) uncooked millet
2 cups (470 ml) milk of choice
1½ cups (355 ml) water
1½ cups (220 g) blackberries, divided
½ teaspoon ground ginger
Fine sea salt
3 tablespoons (60 g) honey, plus more for topping
1 teaspoon vanilla extract
2 tablespoons (30 ml) freshly squeezed lemon juice
1 cup (240 g) plain Greek yogurt
Toasted walnuts, chopped
Unsweetened toasted coconut flakes

**Yield: 4 servings**

# Slow Cooker Miso Oat and Egg Bowls

If you have yet to get acquainted with the savory side of steel-cut oats, there is no time like the present to make it happen. And with your slow cooker leading the charge, these warming breakfast bowls could not be easier to get on the table. This recipe calls for sweet white miso for its delicate, umami-rich flavor and the way it makes a humble bowl of oats taste totally indulgent, though feel free to experiment with other varieties of miso.

1 cup (80 g) steel-cut oats
4 cups (940 ml) vegetable broth
3 tablespoons (45 g) white miso
1 tablespoon (14 g) unsalted butter, plus more for greasing the slow cooker
4 large eggs
4 radishes, thinly sliced
Broccoli, clover, or alfalfa sprouts
Toasted pumpkin seeds

**Yield: 4 servings**

Thoroughly coat the insert of a 6-quart (5.4 L) or larger slow cooker with a light layer of butter. Combine the oats and broth in the insert and stir together. Cover and cook on low for 7 to 8 hours.

Stir the oats together once more. Whisk the miso and butter into the oats. Keep the slow cooker on warm while you prepare the eggs.

Bring a medium saucepan of water to a boil over medium heat. Use a spoon to carefully lower the eggs into the water. Cook for 6 minutes, maintaining a gentle boil. Reduce the heat if necessary. Transfer the eggs to an ice bath, until they're cool enough to handle but still warm. Peel the eggs, and slice each one in half.

To serve, divide the oats among bowls. Top with an egg, sliced radish, sprouts, and pumpkin seeds.

**Tip:** Don't skip the ice bath when making boiled eggs. The benefits are twofold: The cold water stops the eggs from cooking any further and it makes them much easier to peel.

# Spinach and Mushroom Pesto Breakfast Bowls

While basil pesto is suggested with this bowl combination, feel free to make it with any of your favorite herbs. Even greens like arugula or kale would make a fine choice. Pesto is a great sauce to make in advance and stash in the freezer, so you always have some on hand. Even the mushrooms and spinach can be sautéed ahead of time, then reheated or simply added to the bowl chilled.

Heat 1 tablespoon (15 ml) of the oil in a large skillet over medium-high heat. Add the mushrooms and season with salt and pepper. Cook, stirring occasionally, until well browned, about 5 minutes. Transfer to a plate and set aside.

Heat another tablespoon (15 ml) of oil in the same pan over medium heat. Add the spinach. Cook, tossing occasionally, until wilted, about 2 minutes. Transfer to the plate with the mushrooms. Heat the remaining 1 tablespoon (15 ml) oil in the skillet and fry the eggs.

Toss the zucchini noodles with a spoonful of pesto. To serve, divide the zucchini noodles among bowls. Add the mushrooms, spinach, fried egg, and avocado. Top with extra pesto and sprinkle with red pepper flakes.

3 tablespoons (45 ml) avocado or
    extra-virgin olive oil, divided
16 cremini mushrooms, quartered
Kosher salt and freshly ground pepper
8 packed cups (240 g) baby spinach
4 large eggs
8 ounces (225 g) zucchini noodles
½ cup (120 ml) Simple Pesto (page 156)
2 avocados, peeled, pitted, and diced
Red pepper flakes

**Yield: 4 servings**

# Slow Cooker Congee Breakfast Bowls

Congee is a simple, ultra-comforting, and nourishing rice porridge that cooks low and slow until the grains of rice break down and become creamy. Here, it's infused with a few coins of fresh ginger and a few cups of stock for a more savory flavor. In the time it takes your coffee to brew, you can give the vegetables a quick sauté and fry a couple of eggs.

¾ cup (125 g) jasmine rice

4 cups (940 ml) water

3 cups (705 ml) vegetable stock

1-inch (2.5 cm) piece fresh ginger, peeled and thinly sliced

Kosher salt and freshly ground black pepper

3 tablespoons (45 ml) avocado or extra-virgin olive oil, divided

6 ounces (168 g) mushrooms, preferably cremini or shiitake, sliced

6 cups (180 g) baby spinach

4 large eggs

Kimchi (see Note)

Scallions, thinly sliced

**Yield: 4 servings**

**Note:** Many traditional versions of kimchi contain shellfish products, so if you're avoiding shellfish, look for a jar of vegetarian or vegan kimchi.

Add the rice, water, stock, ginger, and 1 teaspoon salt to a 3½-quart (3.2 L) or larger slow cooker and stir together. Cover, set to low, and cook until the rice is broken down and creamy, about 8 hours.

Remove and discard the ginger. Stir, scraping the sides and bottom of the slow cooker. Divide the congee among bowls.

Heat 1 tablespoon (15 ml) of the oil in a large skillet over medium-high heat. Add the mushrooms, season with salt and pepper, and sauté until tender, about 5 minutes. Spoon over the congee.

Heat 1 tablespoon (15 ml) of oil in the same skillet over medium heat. Add the spinach and cook, tossing occasionally, until just wilted, about 2 minutes. Divide the spinach among the bowls.

Heat the remaining 1 tablespoon (15 ml) oil in the same skillet, and fry the eggs.

Add the eggs to the bowls of congee, and top with kimchi and scallions.

# Buckwheat and Black Bean Breakfast Bowls

This bowl is a gathering of all the favorite avocado toast toppings, like dark leafy greens, protein-rich beans, briny feta crumbles, and a dash of heat. But unlike avocado toast, this breakfast can be prepped entirely ahead of time, so all that's left to do in the morning is mash the avocado and pile everything into your favorite bowl.

Combine the buckwheat, water, butter, and a generous pinch of salt and ground black pepper in a medium saucepan. Bring to a boil, then reduce the heat to low, cover, and simmer until tender, 15 to 20 minutes.

To serve, divide the buckwheat among bowls. Top with the steamed kale, beans, sliced hard-boiled egg, avocado, radish, and feta. Drizzle with Miso-Ginger Sauce and sprinkle with sesame seeds and Aleppo pepper.

¾ cup (125 g) kasha buckwheat
1⅓ cups (315 ml) water
½ tablespoon (7 g) unsalted butter
Kosher salt and freshly ground black pepper
4 cups (520 g) steamed kale
1½ cups (300 g) or 1 can (15 ounces, or 420 g) black beans, drained and rinsed
4 hard-boiled eggs
2 avocados, peeled, pitted, and mashed
1 watermelon radish, thinly sliced
Crumbled feta
1 recipe Miso-Ginger Sauce (page 172)
Sesame seeds
Aleppo pepper

**Yield: 4 servings**

# Bacon and Egg Breakfast Burger

Imitation bacon bits and tofu eggs go together like peanut butter and jelly in this burger that knocks the socks off any fast food breakfast sammy. When you're on the go, eat this on a whole wheat bun or an English muffin, with a slice of cheese or a little garlic mayo. At home you can add a side of hash browns or home fries. Garnish with your favorite breakfast toppings (think omelet here: diced and grilled peppers and onions, salsa, ketchup, avocado, or spinach).

12 ounces (340 g) extra-firm tofu, drained and pressed (See Tip on page 59.)
¼ teaspoon ground turmeric
1 tablespoon (8 g) garlic powder
1 tablespoon (8 g) onion powder
1 tablespoon (15 g) yellow mustard
¼ teaspoon sea salt
¼ cup (25 g) imitation bacon bits, store-bought or homemade (page 176)
½ to 1 cup (62 to 125 g) all-purpose flour
2 tablespoons (30 ml) oil, for frying

**Yield: 4 burgers**

Crumble the tofu into a large mixing bowl.

Add the turmeric, garlic powder, onion powder, mustard, salt, and bacon bits, and stir to combine.

Knead in the flour a little at a time. Depending on how much moisture was left in your tofu, you may need a little or a lot. Knead the heck out of this until you get a nice ball of dough, at least 5 minutes.

Let sit for at least 15 minutes to rest. Divide the dough into 4 equal parts and form into patties.

Panfry in the oil for 4 to 5 minutes per side, or until nice and golden brown.

# Cherry Oatmeal Protein-Packed Energy Burger

They may look like cookies, but they're ultra portable and will keep you satisfied all the way 'til lunchtime. Instead of a glass of milk to wash down this cookie (er, burger!), blend up a smoothie: add frozen pineapple, mango, spinach, a scoop of your favorite protein powder and blend together with coconut milk.

Preheat the oven to 350°F (180°C, or gas mark 4). Line a baking sheet with parchment or a silicone baking mat.

In a large mixing bowl, combine the flours, oats, dried cherries, protein powder, brown sugar, cashews, wheat germ, pumpkin seeds, sunflower seeds, baking powder, baking soda, salt, and cinnamon.

In a separate bowl, whisk together the yogurt, milk, nut butter, agave, and coconut oil.

Add the dry ingredients to the wet and mix well, using your hands, until a nice dough forms.

Divide into 8 portions. Form into patties. Place on the prepared baking sheet.

Bake, uncovered, for 18 to 20 minutes, or until the tops just start to crack.

½ cup (80 g) rice flour
½ cup (56 g) coconut flour
1 cup (80 g) quick-cooking oats
1 cup (120 g) dried cherries or your favorite dried fruit
½ cup (92 g) pea protein powder
½ cup (110 g) firmly packed brown sugar
½ cup (65 g) raw cashews or nut of choice
¼ cup (29 g) wheat germ
¼ cup (32 g) hulled pumpkin seeds
¼ cup (32 g) hulled sunflower seeds
½ teaspoon baking powder
½ teaspoon baking soda
½ teaspoon sea salt
½ teaspoon ground cinnamon
1 container (6 ounces, or 170 g) vanilla-flavored yogurt
½ cup (120 ml) milk of choice
¼ cup (64 g) cashew nut butter
¼ cup (84 g) agave nectar
¼ cup (60 ml melted or 56 g solid) coconut oil

**Yield: 8 burgers**

*2*

# HEARTY SOUPS

There's no doubt you can make soup all year round, whether they're brothy soups, chunky soups, vegetable soups, bean soups, noodle soups, winter soups, or summer soups. Soup is a great way to use up ingredients that are hanging out in the back of your fridge. It's also a great way to pack in a lot of nutrition from a variety of vegetables. The soups in this chapter are definite go-tos for comforting, filling, healthy, and flavorful bowls of goodness.

# Easy Black Bean Soup

This quick and easy soup needs just thirty minutes to get a punch of flavor. Packed with healthy plant-based protein, vegetables, and spices, this cozy meal is perfect for a weeknight. Try it with macaroni noodles.

2 tablespoons (28 ml) olive oil

1 yellow onion, diced

2 cloves garlic, minced

1 red bell pepper, diced

1 teaspoon ground cumin

½ teaspoon dried oregano

½ teaspoon smoked paprika

½ teaspoon salt, or to taste

3 cans (15 ounces, or 425 g each) black beans, rinsed and drained (or 4 cups [688 g] cooked beans)

1 can (14.5 ounces, or 410 g) diced tomatoes

3–4 cups (700–935 ml) low-sodium vegetable broth

FOR SERVING (OPTIONAL):

Diced avocado

Sliced scallion

Chopped tomato

Fresh lime juice

Hot pepper sauce

Crushed tortilla chips

**Yield: 4 to 6 servings**

In a soup pot over medium heat, heat the olive oil and sauté the onion for 5 to 6 minutes until softened and translucent. Add the garlic and bell pepper and sauté for 2 to 3 minutes. Add the cumin, oregano, smoked paprika, and salt and sauté for another 1 to 2 minutes until the spices are fragrant.

Add the black beans, tomatoes, and 3 cups (700 ml) of vegetable broth. You can add more broth later if you like a thinner soup. Bring to a boil. Reduce the heat to low and simmer for 15 to 20 minutes.

Using an immersion blender, purée half of the soup. Alternatively, you can carefully transfer half of the soup to a blender, purée, and add it back to the pot. Add the other cup (235 ml) of broth if you like a thinner soup.

Serve hot with the toppings of your choice.

# Creamy Tomato Soup with Orzo

Tomato soup is a staple. It's great as a combo with sandwiches or salads, but this version is hearty enough to stand alone. White beans add fiber and protein, but they are puréed into the soup so no one will ever know they're in there. Orzo pasta adds bulk and a bit of fun. Serve with garlic bread or a slice of crusty bread.

In a large soup pot, heat the olive oil over medium-high heat. Add the onion and sauté for 4 to 5 minutes until soft and translucent. Add the garlic, cumin, and basil. Sauté for 1 minute until fragrant.

Add the cannellini beans, crushed tomatoes, balsamic vinegar, salt, and 2 cups (475 ml) of vegetable broth. Raise the heat to high to bring to a boil and then reduce the heat to medium-low and simmer for 10 minutes.

Using an immersion blender, purée the soup until smooth. Alternatively, you can carefully transfer the soup to a blender, in batches if necessary, blend until smooth, and return it to the soup pot.

Add the orzo and remaining 1 cup (235 ml) of vegetable broth. Stir. Bring the soup back to a boil over high heat and then reduce to a simmer again over medium-low heat and simmer for 10 to 12 minutes until the orzo is tender, stirring occasionally to prevent sticking.

2 tablespoons (28 ml) olive oil
1 sweet onion, diced
2 cloves garlic, minced
1 teaspoon ground cumin
2 teaspoons dried basil
1 can (15 ounces, or 425 g) cannellini beans (white kidney beans), drained and rinsed
1 can (28 ounces, or 785 g) crushed tomatoes
2 tablespoons balsamic vinegar
1 teaspoon salt, or to taste
3 cups (710 ml) low-sodium vegetable broth, divided
½ cup (84 g) uncooked orzo

**Yield: 4 servings**

# Easy Minestrone with Macaroni Noodles

This soup is hearty and flavorful and reminiscent of a grandmother's Sunday soup, although a bit healthier. Because it's made with nearly all staple ingredients, it can easily be a go-to meal any night of the week.

1 tablespoon (15 ml) olive oil
½ sweet onion, peeled and diced
2 cloves garlic, peeled and minced
1 package (16 ounces, or 455 g) frozen mixed vegetables
1 can (28 ounces, or 785 g) crushed tomatoes
4 cups (946 ml) low-sodium vegetable broth
1 tablespoon (1 g) dried parsley
1 teaspoon dried oregano
½ teaspoon dried thyme
1 teaspoon salt, or to taste
⅛ teaspoon black pepper, or to taste
1 can (15 ounces, or 425 g) red kidney beans, rinsed and drained (or 1½ cups [266 g] cooked beans)
1 cup (67 g) chopped kale leaves or spinach
2 cups (280 g) cooked macaroni noodles
1 tablespoon (4 g) nutritional yeast (optional)

**Yield: 4 servings**

Heat the olive oil in a soup pot over medium heat. Sauté the onion and garlic for 4 to 5 minutes until translucent and soft. Add the frozen vegetables, crushed tomatoes, vegetable broth, parsley, oregano, thyme, salt, and pepper. Simmer for 20 minutes to allow the vegetables to become tender and the flavors to mingle.

Add the kidney beans, kale, and noodles and simmer for another 2 to 3 minutes to warm through. Take off the heat. Add the nutritional yeast, if using, and stir.

# Creamy Potato Soup with Kale and Corn

Everyone, from adults to teens to kids, loves this soup. It's thick, creamy, and hearty, and it's loaded with healthy vegetables. (The secret is celery salt.) You'll love it, too.

Heat the olive oil in a soup pot over medium heat. Sauté the onion and garlic for 4 to 5 minutes until they begin to soften. Add the carrot and celery and sauté for 3 to 4 more minutes. Add the vegetable broth, potatoes, dill, celery salt, salt, and pepper. Increase the heat to bring to a boil, reduce the heat to low, and simmer for 15 minutes until the potatoes are tender.

Using an immersion blender, purée about one-quarter to one-third of the soup to create a thick creamy base. Alternatively, take about 2 cups (475 ml) of the soup and carefully purée it in a blender and then return it to the soup pot.

Add the corn and kale, if using, stir to combine, and simmer for 5 more minutes to heat through. Take off the heat and add the coconut milk, if using.

Serve with a few dashes of sriracha or hot pepper sauce, if desired.

2 tablespoons (28 ml) olive oil

½ onion, diced

2 cloves garlic, minced

1 carrot, peeled and diced

2 ribs celery, diced

3 cups (700 ml) low-sodium vegetable broth

4 cups (440 g) diced potatoes, peeled (about 5 to 6 medium-size)

½ teaspoon dried dill

½ teaspoon celery salt

½ teaspoon salt, or to taste

¼ teaspoon black pepper, or to taste

½ cup (77 g) fresh or (82 g) frozen corn kernels

1 cup (67 g) chopped kale, woody stems removed (optional)

¼ cup (60 ml) lite coconut milk (optional)

Sriracha or hot pepper sauce (optional)

**Yield: 4 servings**

# Miso Soup with Shiitake Mushrooms and Ramen Noodles

This soup is everything: cozy, comforting, healthy, easy, and so delicious. Make it when you feel yourself coming down with a cold. It's soothing and nourishing.

1 tablespoon (15 ml) olive oil, plus more if needed

2 cloves garlic, minced

1-inch (2.5 cm) piece fresh ginger, peeled and minced

8 ounces (225 g) shiitake mushrooms, stems removed, caps thinly sliced

4 tablespoons (64 g) mellow white miso paste

2 tablespoons (28 ml) tamari

½ teaspoon ground turmeric

8 cups (1.9 L) low-sodium vegetable broth

6 ounces (170 g) instant ramen noodles

3 collard leaves or lacinato kale, chiffonade

Sriracha or hot pepper sauce (optional)

**Yield: 4 to 6 servings**

Heat the olive oil in a large soup pot over medium heat. Add the garlic and ginger and sauté for 1 minute until fragrant.

Add the mushrooms, stir, and sauté for 5 to 6 minutes. The mushrooms should give off some of their own liquid, but if the pot seems too dry, add another tablespoon (15 ml) of olive oil or a few tablespoons (60 ml) of vegetable broth.

Add the miso, tamari, and turmeric and stir to coat the mushrooms. Add the vegetable broth, raise the heat to bring to a boil, and then reduce the heat to low and simmer for 15 minutes.

Add the instant ramen noodles and collard leaves and simmer for another 3 to 5 minutes until the noodles are tender.

Serve with a few dashes of sriracha or hot pepper sauce in each bowl, if desired.

**Tip:** For a gluten-free option, use 4 ounces (115 g) thin rice noodles instead of the ramen.

# Mixed Lentil Quinoa Soup

Two kinds of lentils are the secret to the substance of this soup. The red lentils cook quickly and nearly disappear into the soup, giving it body, while the green lentils retain their shape and offer texture.

Heat the olive oil in a large soup pot over medium heat. Add the onion and sauté for 4 to 5 minutes until softened and translucent. Add the garlic, celery, and carrots and sauté for 3 to 4 minutes until starting to soften.

Add the remaining ingredients, except the fresh parsley. Increase the heat to high to bring to a boil and then reduce the heat to medium-low. Simmer for 35 to 40 minutes until the lentils are tender, stirring occasionally to prevent sticking. The red lentils should be unrecognizable as they will break down and become part of the soup base.

Add the chopped parsley and stir through just before serving.

2 tablespoons (28 ml) olive oil

1 yellow onion, diced

2 cloves garlic, minced

2 ribs celery, diced

2 carrots, peeled and diced

1 cup (192 g) dry red lentils, picked over and rinsed well with cold water

1 cup (192 g) dry brown or green lentils, picked over and rinsed well with cold water

½ cup (87 g) dry quinoa, rinsed well with cold water

1 can (28 ounces, or 785 g) diced tomatoes

6 cups (1.4 L) low-sodium vegetable broth

2 tablespoons (28 ml) tamari, coconut aminos, or soy sauce

1 tablespoon (7 g) ground cumin

1 tablespoon (7 g) smoked paprika

1 teaspoon dried thyme

1 teaspoon dried oregano

1 teaspoon salt, or to taste

½ teaspoon dried basil

½ teaspoon ground nutmeg

Handful of fresh parsley, chopped (about ¼ cup [15 g] loosely packed, before chopping)

**Yield: 6 servings**

# Tuscan White Bean Soup

This is such a comforting, warming soup. Creamy white beans make it hearty and filling, yet light tasting. Superfood kale mingles with familiar vegetables like carrots, celery, and tomatoes. Chop the kale leaves really small; this allows the kale to soften quickly and makes it easy to eat. Serve this soup with a big hunk of crusty bread.

2 tablespoons (28 ml) olive oil

1 yellow onion, diced

3 cloves garlic, minced

1 cup (130 g) diced carrots (about 3 medium carrots)

2 ribs celery, diced

2 tablespoons (28 ml) white wine vinegar

1 teaspoon dried thyme

1 teaspoon dried oregano

½ teaspoon dried basil

2 teaspoons salt, or to taste

¼ teaspoon black pepper, or to taste

2 tablespoons (28 ml) tamari, coconut aminos, or soy sauce

1 can (15 ounces, or 425 g) diced tomatoes

2 cans (15 ounces, or 425 g each) cannellini beans (white kidney beans), drained and rinsed

6 cups (1.4 L) low-sodium vegetable broth

3-4 kale leaves, stems removed, chopped small

¼ cup (15 g) loosely packed fresh parsley, chopped

**Yield: 4 to 6 servings**

Heat the olive oil in a large soup pot over medium heat. Add the onion and sauté for 5 to 6 minutes until soft and translucent. Add the garlic, carrots, celery, and white wine vinegar. Sauté for 3 to 4 minutes until the vegetables are starting to soften and the vinegar is mostly absorbed.

Add the thyme, oregano, basil, salt, pepper, tamari, tomatoes, cannellini beans, and vegetable broth. Increase the heat to high and bring to a boil and then reduce the heat to low and simmer for 15 to 20 minutes.

Add the kale and parsley. Stir to combine and heat through.

## 3

# SATISFYING SALADS

Salads don't have to be boring plates of lettuce. They are a great way to offer a variety of healthy vegetables, but they can also include fruits, pasta, beans, grains, nuts, and seeds. Smaller serving sizes of the salads in this chapter can be sides or starters, but don't be afraid to fill a big bowl and eat a salad as a meal.

# Very Berry Quinoa Salad with Cinnamon Toasted Pecans

This salad is light and fresh yet has plenty of protein from the quinoa and pecans. Fresh summer berries are little powerhouses of vitamins and add a touch of bright sweetness. The toasted pecans take this dish to the next level.

**For the Quinoa:** Combine the quinoa and water in a small pot and bring to a boil. Cover, reduce the heat to medium-low, and simmer for 12 to 15 minutes until the quinoa is tender and the liquid is absorbed. Fluff with a fork.

**For the Cinnamon Toasted Pecans:** Line a large plate with parchment paper and set aside. In a small bowl, whisk together the maple syrup, sugar, cinnamon, and salt. Add the pecans and stir to coat evenly.

Heat the coconut oil in a nonstick skillet over medium heat. Pour the pecans in the skillet, spreading them out in an even layer. Cook for 4 to 5 minutes, stirring frequently, until toasted. Nuts can burn quickly, so don't walk away at this point! You'll know the pecans are done when you start to smell them. Pour them out onto the parchment-lined plate and spread in an even layer. Let them cool. They will crisp up as they cool.

**For the Salad:** Combine the mixed baby greens, mixed berries, cooked quinoa, and toasted pecans in a large salad bowl. Mix well. To serve, divide among 4 bowls and drizzle with the Maple Dijon Vinaigrette.

FOR QUINOA:
1 cup (173 g) tri-color dry quinoa, rinsed
    well with cold water (or any color
    quinoa, see page 7)
1¼ cups (295 ml) water

FOR CINNAMON TOASTED PECANS:
1½ tablespoons (30 g) pure maple syrup
1 tablespoon (9 g) coconut sugar or
    (15 g) brown sugar
½ teaspoon ground cinnamon
Pinch of salt
1 cup (110 g) pecan halves
1 teaspoon coconut oil

FOR SALAD:
6 cups (330 g) mixed baby salad greens
2 cups (weight will vary) fresh mixed
    berries (blueberries, blackberries,
    raspberries, strawberries, etc.)
1 recipe Maple Dijon Vinaigrette
    (page 170)

**Yield: 4 servings**

**Note:** Try using romaine, red leaf lettuce, or arugula instead of the mixed baby greens to change it up.

# Black Bean Citrus Quinoa Salad

This salad is light and bright with fresh veggies and citrus, yet the quinoa and black beans make it incredibly filling. Take this dish to potlucks and watch it disappear.

1 cup (173 g) dry quinoa, rinsed well with cold water
1¼ cups (295 ml) water
¼ cup (60 ml) extra-virgin olive oil
¼ cup (60 ml) fresh lime juice
1 tablespoon (15 ml) apple cider vinegar
¼ teaspoon salt, or to taste
⅛ teaspoon black pepper, or to taste
1 can (15 ounces, or 425 g) black beans, drained and rinsed
1 English cucumber, diced
1 pint (275 g) grape tomatoes, halved
¼ cup (40 g) diced red onion
4 mandarin oranges (such as clementines), peeled and segmented

**Yield: 4 to 6 servings**

**Note:** You may chop up a head of romaine lettuce and toss it with the rest of the ingredients, making it stretch even further.

Add the quinoa and water to a pot on the stove and bring to a boil. Cover, reduce the heat to medium-low, and simmer for 12 to 15 minutes until the water is absorbed and the quinoa is tender. Fluff with a fork.

Meanwhile, whisk together the olive oil, lime juice, apple cider vinegar, salt, and pepper. Set aside.

Add the cooked quinoa to a large mixing bowl and add the black beans, cucumber, tomatoes, onion, and mandarin oranges. Pour in the dressing and mix well to combine.

This salad can be eaten immediately, at room temperature, or cold.

# Black Bean and Rice Kale Salad

In this salad, you make an avocado dressing to massage into the kale, which softens it as it coats it. Then you top off the whole thing with a generous dollop of protein-packed hummus. Avocado and hummus might seem like a strange combo at first, but really, it's so good.

Whisk or blend together one half of the avocado, lemon juice, salt, pepper, turmeric, and olive oil. Pour over the kale in a large bowl. Mix it around well so the dressing covers all the kale. Now, with clean hands, get in there and massage the dressing into the kale by rubbing the leaves for about 2 minutes. This will soften the kale to make it easier to chew and make it more flavorful.

Dice the remaining half of the avocado and add it to the kale along with the cooked brown rice, black beans, tomatoes, and Quick Pickled Red Onions and toss to combine.

**For the Hummus:** In a food processor, combine all the ingredients, except the water, and purée until smooth. Add water, 1 tablespoon (15 ml) at a time, until the desired consistency is reached.

Portion the salad out in individual bowls and top each one with a generous dollop of Hummus.

1 avocado, peel and pit removed, halves divided
Juice of ½ lemon, plus more to taste
½ teaspoon salt, or to taste
¼ teaspoon black pepper, or to taste
¼ teaspoon ground turmeric
⅓ cup (80 ml) extra-virgin olive oil
1 bunch kale, woody stems removed, chopped into small bite-size pieces
1 cup (195 g) cooked brown rice
1 can (15 ounces, or 425 g) black beans, drained and rinsed
2 tomatoes, diced
½ cup (160 g) Quick Pickled Red Onions (page 178)
1½ cups (370 g) Hummus (recipe below or store-bought)

FOR HUMMUS:
1 can (15 ounces, or 425 g) chickpeas, drained and rinsed
1 clove garlic
2 tablespoons (30 g) tahini
½ teaspoon ground cumin
2 tablespoons (28 ml) fresh lemon juice
½ teaspoon salt, or to taste
2 tablespoons (28 ml) extra-virgin olive oil
Water to thin as needed

**Yield: 4 to 6 servings**

**Note:** Any grains would work in this salad in place of the rice—quinoa, couscous, millet, or farro. Use whatever you have left over in your fridge.

# Cherry Almond Couscous Salad with Butternut Squash and Apples

This recipe is inspired by a Stuffed Acorn Squash recipe in the cookbook *Vegan Yum Yum* by Lauren Ulm. Instead of using the couscous as a stuffing, the squash is diced along with some apples for a sweet and tart contrast and then mixed with the couscous all together in one bowl over healthy greens.

2½ cups (350 g) diced butternut squash (about 1-inch [2.5 cm] size cubes)

2 teaspoons olive oil

¾ teaspoon salt, or to taste, divided

¼ teaspoon black pepper, or to taste

½ teaspoon ground cinnamon

½ cup (80 g) dried cherries

½ cup (73 g) raw almonds, whole or chopped as desired

1½ cups (355 ml) water

1 cup (175 g) dry couscous

4 cups (120 g) baby spinach or greens of choice

1 tart apple, chopped

2 scallions, sliced

1 recipe Maple Dijon Vinaigrette (page 170)

**Yield: 4 servings**

Preheat the oven to 400°F (200°C, or gas mark 6). Line a rimmed baking sheet with parchment paper and set aside.

Toss the butternut squash with olive oil, ¼ teaspoon of salt, pepper, and cinnamon. Mix well to coat evenly. Spread onto the prepared baking sheet in one even layer. Roast for 15 minutes, gently stir the squash and spread back out in an even layer, and roast for 10 more minutes until tender.

Meanwhile, place the dried cherries, almonds, and water in a pot on the stove. Bring to a boil, add the couscous, cover, and remove from the heat. Let sit for 5 minutes and then fluff with a fork.

Toss the spinach, apple, and scallions in a salad bowl. Top with the couscous mixture and roasted butternut squash. Drizzle with the Maple Dijon Vinaigrette (you may not use it all) and toss to coat evenly.

**Tip:** Prechopped butternut squash is fairly easy to find in grocery stores these days. It's a great time-saver!

*4*

# LOADED HANDHELD SNACKS

Sandwiches aren't just for lunch boxes! The ingredient possibilities are endless—just about anything can be packed between two slices of bread, stuffed into a pita or wrap, folded up in a tortilla, or laid out open-face as a pizza or baguette. Many of these "snacks" are suitable for a lunch box (or brown paper bag), but all of them make yummy dinners. And who doesn't love to eat with their hands?

# Spicy Hummus Veggie Wraps

It doesn't get much easier than using store-bought coleslaw or broccoli slaw mix. There's wonderful flavor contrast between the spicy hummus, the sweet apple, and the tangy slaw. This wrap also has texture contrast between the hummus, slaw, apple, and tortilla. Feel free to add a sprinkle of sunflower seeds or crushed walnuts for extra protein and crunch.

**FOR SPICY HUMMUS:**

1 can (15 ounces, or 425 g) chickpeas, drained and rinsed (or 1½ cups [246 g] cooked chickpeas)

1 clove garlic

2 tablespoons (30 g) tahini

½ teaspoon ground cumin

2 tablespoons (28 ml) fresh lemon juice

¼ teaspoon salt, or to taste

¼ cup (65 g) spicy salsa

**FOR VEGGIE WRAPS:**

2 cups (200 g) coleslaw mix or broccoli slaw mix

¼ cup (60 g) plain yogurt

1 tablespoon (15 ml) fresh lemon juice

Dash of salt and black pepper, or to taste

4 large tortillas (gluten-free, if desired)

1 cup (246 g) Spicy Hummus or store-bought

2 big handfuls of baby spinach or leafy green of choice

1 crisp apple, sliced thin

**Yield: 4 servings**

**For the Spicy Hummus:** Place all the ingredients in the bowl of a food processor. Process until smooth, stopping the machine and scraping down the sides occasionally, if needed.

**For the Veggie Wraps:** Mix the coleslaw mix, yogurt, lemon juice, salt, and pepper in a mixing bowl. Set aside.

Lay out one tortilla on a clean flat surface. Spread about ¼ cup (62 g) of Spicy Hummus all over the surface of the tortilla. Place some spinach leaves on top of the Spicy Hummus. On half of the tortilla, pile ½ cup (50 g) of the coleslaw mix and one-quarter of the apple slices.

Fold in the sides of the tortilla and then, starting with the end that has the slaw and apples, roll tightly. Cut in half. Repeat with the remaining tortillas and ingredients.

> **Tip:** The Spicy Hummus can be made ahead of time and kept covered in the fridge for several days. Don't be afraid to use a spicy salsa for this recipe as the other ingredients will help to mellow out the heat.

# Curried Tofu Salad Sandwiches

Crumbled firm tofu, crisp celery, and juicy apples mingle among a creamy, tangy curry dressing. It's perfect on its own, with crackers, or piled high on a sandwich. Quick and easy to make—and it's even better the next day.

In a medium mixing bowl, whisk the yogurt, mayo, Dijon mustard, lemon juice, curry powder, turmeric, salt, and pepper.

With your clean hands, crumble the tofu in the same bowl. Don't be perfect; leave some pieces bigger than others and crumble some pieces smaller. This will help give the salad extra texture.

Add the celery, apple, scallions, and parsley to the tofu. Mix well until everything is well covered in the creamy curry dressing.

You can enjoy this right away or store it in the fridge to let the flavors come together even more.

When ready to eat, toast the bread, if desired. Pile about ½ cup (130 g) of the curried tofu onto one slice of bread. Add lettuce and tomato, if desired. Top with another slice of bread.

½ cup (85 g) unsweetened plain yogurt
2 tablespoons (28 g) mayo
1 tablespoon (15 g) Dijon mustard
1 tablespoon (15 ml) fresh lemon juice
2½ teaspoons (5 g) yellow curry powder
½ teaspoon ground turmeric
½ teaspoon salt, or to taste
⅛ teaspoon black pepper, or to taste
1 package (14 ounces, or 390 g) firm or extra-firm tofu, drained and pressed (see Tip)
1 rib celery, diced
1 sweet apple, cored and diced
2 scallions, diced
1 tablespoon (4 g) chopped fresh parsley
12 slices bread
Lettuce and tomato slices, for serving (optional)

**Yield: 6 sandwiches**

**Tip:** To press the tofu, wrap the block of tofu in several paper towels or a clean kitchen towel and place on a plate. Place another plate on top of the tofu and weigh down the top plate. Cans or bags of beans or rice work well for this or a heavy skillet. This tower may start to topple as the tofu loses liquid, so don't use anything breakable, like glass jars, as a weight. Press for about 20 minutes.

**Note:** To make this soy-free, use 2 cans (15 ounces, or 425 g each) of chickpeas, drained and rinsed, instead of tofu. Smash them with a potato masher or fork.

# Falafel Pitas with Quick Pickled Red Onions and Lemon-Dill-Tahini Sauce

These easy falafel pitas are loaded with flavor and texture. They're fresh, creamy, crunchy, and savory. If you're sending this as a lunch, keep the components separate and assemble when ready to eat.

**For the Falafel:** Heat 1 tablespoon (15 ml) of olive oil in a small skillet over medium heat. Add the onion and garlic and sauté for 4 to 5 minutes until soft.

In the bowl of a food processor, add the sautéed onions and garlic along with all the remaining falafel ingredients, except the remaining olive oil. Pulse until well combined, but NOT puréed. The mixture should be a bit chunky. It may look loose and crumbly but should hold together well when pressed in your hand.

Form 2 tablespoons (28 g) of the falafel mixture into a ball with your hands and flatten into a patty. Set aside. Repeat with the remaining falafel mixture. You should have 11 to 12 falafel patties.

Wipe out the skillet you used for the onions and garlic and heat another tablespoon (15 ml) of oil over medium heat. Add half of the falafel patties and cook for 3 to 4 minutes until golden brown on the bottom. Gently flip them over and cook for another 3 to 4 minutes until golden brown on the second side. Add the final tablespoon of olive oil (15 ml) and repeat with the remaining falafel patties.

**For the Lemon-Dill-Tahini Sauce:** Whisk all the ingredients in a small bowl. Taste and adjust the seasoning.

To assemble the pita pockets: Add a leaf or two of lettuce to one pita pocket, followed by a slice or two of tomato, 2 to 3 slices of cucumber, 2 to 3 falafel patties, and several slices of Quick Pickled Red Onions. Drizzle with the Lemon-Dill-Tahini Sauce.

**FOR FALAFEL:**
3 tablespoons (45 ml) olive oil, divided
½ red onion, diced
3 cloves garlic, minced
1 can (15 ounces, or 425 g) chickpeas, drained and rinsed (or 1½ cups [246 g] cooked chickpeas)
¼ cup (15 g) fresh parsley
¼ cup (4 g) fresh cilantro
2 tablespoons (16 g) sesame seeds
1 teaspoon ground cumin
1 teaspoon coriander
½ teaspoon turmeric
½ teaspoon paprika
½ teaspoon salt, or to taste
⅓ cup (30 g) chickpea flour (All-purpose flour or a gluten-free flour blend will work as well.)

**FOR LEMON-DILL-TAHINI SAUCE:**
½ cup (115 g) plain yogurt
2 tablespoons (30 g) tahini
Juice of ½ lemon
½ teaspoon garlic powder, or to taste
¼ teaspoon salt, or to taste
1 tablespoon (4 g) chopped fresh dill

**FOR PITA POCKETS:**
4 pita pocket halves
Green leaf lettuce
Sliced tomatoes
Sliced cucumbers
Quick Pickled Red Onions (page 178)

**Yield: 4 servings**

# Smashed Black Bean Green Chile Quesadillas

Quesadillas are a terrific go-to meal when you're short on time and have nothing planned. Leftovers smashed in a tortilla and panfried until crisp instantly become a delicious dinner that everyone wants to eat. Bonus points if you serve it with a dipping sauce. No leftovers? No problem. Quesadillas don't require much work to make them taste amazing, even from scratch. Serve with a simple green salad on the side to complete this meal.

---

1 can (15 ounces, or 425 g) black beans, drained and rinsed
1 can (4.5 ounces, or 130 g) mild diced green chiles
1½ teaspoons ground cumin
1 teaspoon fine salt, or to taste
1 recipe Sharp Salsa Queso Dip (page 176)
5–6 flour tortillas (9 or 10 inches, or 23 or 26 cm each) (see Note)
Cooking spray

**Yield: 4 to 6 servings**

**Note:** You may use gluten-free tortillas if desired but note that corn tortillas don't bend well and may break.

In a small bowl, mix the black beans, green chiles, cumin, and salt. Using a potato masher or a fork, smash about half of the mixture. Set aside.

Lay one of the tortillas on a clean flat surface and spread 1 tablespoon (16 g) of Sharp Salsa Queso Dip on half of the tortilla, leaving a little space along the edge. Spread 3 tablespoons (45 g) of bean mixture over the top on the same side. Fold the other side over on top of the filling and press down gently to secure. Avoid pressing too hard as the filling will squish out. Repeat with the remaining tortillas.

Lightly spray a large nonstick skillet with cooking spray and heat over medium-high heat. Once hot, place two tortillas in the pan next to each other. Cook for 3 to 4 minutes until lightly browned and crispy on the bottom. Flip the quesadillas over and cook for another 2 to 3 minutes until the second side is also lightly browned.

Remove the quesadillas to a large plate or cutting board, in a single layer so they stay crispy. Repeat with the remaining quesadillas, spraying the pan again with cooking spray if it is dry. You may need to adjust the heat as you go, reducing the heat to medium if they are browning too much or too quickly.

Once the quesadillas have cooled slightly, slice each one in half or into fourths. Serve with the remaining Sharp Salsa Queso Dip on the side.

# Black Bean Tacos with Corn Radish Salsa and Pickled Red Onions

This will become your go-to taco recipe. It's so easy, ready in twenty minutes or less, and made with pantry and fridge staples. Fresh summer sweet corn takes this recipe up a notch, but you can make them all year round with thawed frozen corn and it's still crazy delicious. Serve with tortilla chips and more guacamole.

**For the Black Beans:** Heat the olive oil in a pot over medium heat. Add the onion and sauté for 4 to 5 minutes until soft and translucent. Add the chili powder and cumin and stir. Add the black beans and vegetable broth and simmer for 5 to 10 minutes. Using a potato masher or fork, mash about half of the bean mixture. Add the salt and lime juice. Taste and adjust the seasoning, if necessary. Remove from the heat.

**For the Corn Radish Salsa:** Add all the ingredients to a small bowl and mix well.

**To assemble the tacos:** Fill one tortilla with ¼ cup (43 g) of black beans, 2 tablespoons (32 g) of Corn Radish Salsa, a dollop of BEST Guacamole, and several Quick Pickled Red Onions. Repeat with the remaining tortillas.

**Tip:** Warm the tortillas! Place the stack of tortillas on a microwave-safe plate covered with a just-barely-damp paper towel. Microwave for 30 seconds at a time until warm. Alternatively, you can wrap the stack of tortillas in aluminum foil and warm in a preheated 350°F (180°C, or gas mark 4) oven for 10 to 15 minutes. Do this while you make the beans and everything will be ready at the same time. Substitute corn tortillas if gluten-free.

**FOR BLACK BEANS:**
1 tablespoon (15 ml) olive oil
½ yellow onion, diced
1 tablespoon (8 g) chili powder
1 teaspoon ground cumin
2 cans (15 ounces, or 425 g each) black beans, drained and rinsed (or 3 cups [516 g] cooked beans)
½ cup (120 ml) low-sodium vegetable broth
¼ teaspoon salt, or to taste
Juice of ½ lime, or more to taste

**FOR CORN RADISH SALSA:**
1 cup (164 g) fresh or thawed corn kernels
2 radishes, diced (about ¼ cup [29 g])
½ jalapeño, diced (ribs and seeds removed)
Juice of ½ lime
½ teaspoon smoked paprika
¼ teaspoon ground cumin
¼ teaspoon salt, or to taste

**FOR TACOS:**
8 soft taco flour tortillas, warmed if desired
BEST Guacamole (page 165)
Quick Pickled Red Onions (page 178)

**Yield: 4 servings, 2 tacos each**

# Rice and Bean Pan-Grilled Burritos with Avocado Green Chile Sauce

A burrito is essentially a taco's much larger and more filling brother. Tacos are generally served with sides to make a complete meal whereas a burrito is a complete meal in itself. Loaded with filling rice, protein-packed beans, fresh crunchy lettuce, and a swoon-worthy sauce, this is one meal that will surely leave you full and satisfied.

**FOR RICE:**
3 cups (585 g) cooked brown rice
¼ cup (4 g) chopped cilantro
1 medium tomato, diced
Juice of ½ lime

**FOR BEANS:**
1 tablespoon (15 ml) olive oil
2 teaspoons ground cumin
½ teaspoon smoked paprika
½ teaspoon chili powder
¼ teaspoon salt, or to taste
¼ teaspoon black pepper
1 can (15 ounces, or 425 g) pinto beans, drained and rinsed (or 1½ cups [257 g] cooked beans)

**FOR AVOCADO GREEN CHILE SAUCE:**
1 avocado, peel and pit removed
1 can (4.5 ounces, or 130 g) mild diced green chiles
Handful of cilantro
Juice of 2–3 limes
¾ teaspoon salt, or to taste
Water to thin, if needed

**FOR BURRITOS:**
1½ cups (71 g) chopped romaine lettuce
Salsa (optional)
6 large (10 inches, or 25 cm each) burrito-size flour tortillas
Cooking spray

**Yield: 6 servings**

**Note:** You may use gluten-free tortillas if desired but note that corn tortillas don't bend well and may break.

**For the Rice:** Mix the cooked brown rice with cilantro, tomato, and lime juice. Stir well.

**For the Beans:** In a small skillet, heat the olive oil over medium heat. Add the cumin, smoked paprika, chili powder, salt, and pepper and stir to make a slurry. Simmer, stirring occasionally, about 1 to 2 minutes until fragrant. Add the pinto beans, stir well, and cook for 2 to 3 minutes to heat through.

**For the Avocado Green Chile Sauce:** Add all the ingredients to a blender and purée until smooth.

**To assemble the burritos:** Wrap the tortillas in a just-damp paper towel and heat in the microwave for 20 to 30 seconds at a time until warm. Lay one tortilla flat and spread ¼ cup (50 g) of Avocado Green Chile Sauce horizontally on one end. Top with a scant one-sixth of rice mixture, ¼ cup (43 g) of beans, ¼ cup (12 g) of romaine lettuce, and a tablespoon or two (16 to 32 g) of salsa, if desired. Fold up the bottom half of the tortilla over the filling, then fold in both sides, and then starting from the bottom, tightly roll up the tortilla to form the burrito. Repeat with the remaining ingredients.

Spray a skillet with cooking spray and heat over medium heat. Working in batches if needed, place the burritos seam-side down and cook for 3 to 4 minutes until lightly seared. The seam should stay closed once seared. Flip the burritos over and cook for another 3 to 4 minutes to sear the second side. You may need to adjust/lower the heat as you go. Watch them closely so they don't burn.

Cut each burrito in half and serve.

# Chicken Salad Sammy

Although there is a lot of tofu in this salad, the real star is the crunch from all the fresh, raw veggies. Serve on a sandwich, in a wrap, or on a bed of greens, or eat it with a fork right out of the bowl.

12 ounces (340 g) extra-firm tofu, drained and pressed (see Tip on page 59.)
2 tablespoons (28 ml) olive oil
4 to 6 cloves garlic, minced
½ cup (54 g) shredded carrot
1 red onion, chopped
2 ribs celery, chopped
½ cup (60 g) walnut pieces
1 cup (150 g) grapes (green or red, or even raisins), halved
1 cup (224 g) mayonnaise, store-bought or homemade vegan (page 161)
Salt and pepper

**Yield: enough for 4 to 6 sandwiches**

Chop up the tofu into tiny, tiny, tiny pieces.

Heat the olive oil in a skillet over medium-high heat and add the garlic. Sauté for a minute. Add the tofu and sauté until golden, 7 to 10 minutes. Remove from the heat and let cool.

Add carrot, onion, celery, walnuts, grapes, mayonnaise, and salt and pepper to taste. Stir to combine.

Chill before serving.

# Pulled "Pork" Sliders

These tasty little plant-based pork sliders will fool the best of them. But why try to fool them?

Oil, for frying
3 cans (20 ounce [565 g] each) young green jackfruit in brine or water, drained, rinsed, and patted dry
3½ cups (825 ml) BBQ sauce (try page 155 or 166)
1 medium yellow onion, julienne cut
12 soft dinner rolls or Hawaiian sweet rolls
1 recipe Creamy BBQ Coleslaw (page 148), prepared

**Yield: 12 sliders**

Heat enough oil to coat the bottom of your frying pan or skillet over medium-high heat.

Add the jackfruit chunks in a single layer and fry until almost completely blackened. This can take up to 10 minutes. Flip and repeat on the other side.

Remove from the heat and allow to cool enough to handle.

Using the tines of a fork, shred the jackfruit until it resembles, well, shredded pork.

Mix the shredded jackfruit, barbecue sauce, and onion together and add to your slow cooker. Cook on medium for 3 hours. Alternatively, use a pot with a tight-fitting lid and simmer, covered, on medium-low heat for 90 minutes, returning every so often to stir.

Split the dinner rolls in half. Pile on equal parts coleslaw and jackfruit and serve.

# Philly Cheesesteak

Serve this classic sandwich on game night to satisfy those sporty cravings.

**To make the cheezy sauce:** Place all the ingredients in a blender or food processor and process until smooth. Place in a saucepan. Heat over low heat until it thickens, constantly stirring so it doesn't get clumpy or scorch.

**To make the sandwiches:** Slice the slider dough into strips about 1 inch (2.5 cm) wide and 4 to 6 inches (10 to 15 cm) long.

In a large frying pan, preheat about 3 tablespoons (45 ml) of oil, adding more later as you continue cooking. Sauté some of the onions, some of the peppers, and some of the slider strips, in amounts you like for your sammies. Season with salt and pepper. Pile high onto the French rolls and drizzle with the cheezy sauce.

**FOR CHEEZY SAUCE:**
2 cups (470 ml) soy creamer
½ cup (60 g) nutritional yeast
½ cup (65 g) raw cashews
1 tablespoon (16 g) tahini
2 tablespoons (36 g) white miso
2 tablespoons (16 g) cornstarch
1 tablespoon (8 g) onion powder
1 tablespoon (8 g) garlic powder
1 tablespoon (8 g) ground mustard

**FOR SANDWICHES:**
Vegetable oil, for frying
2 large white onions, sliced or diced
2 red, green, or yellow bell peppers, sliced into thin strips or diced
½ recipe Green Castle Sliders (See below), prepared but not sliced
Salt and pepper
4 French rolls

**Yield: 4 sandwiches**

# Green Castle Sliders

These are cool because you can refrigerate the logs and slice them up whenever you want a burger. Serve these like the original White Castle sliders with diced white onion, a pickle, and a white bun.

Preheat the oven to 350°F (180°C, or gas mark 4).

In a large bowl, combine the flours, nutritional yeast, black pepper, onion powder, garlic powder, paprika, and cayenne. In a separate bowl, combine the water, oil, tamari, and ketchup.

Add the wet ingredients to the dry and incorporate well. Using your hands, knead the dough for several minutes. Let sit for about 10 minutes.

Divide the dough into 2 equal pieces.

Maneuver the wet mushy mass into a log shape in the center of a large piece of aluminum foil. Roll it tightly into a log, about 2 inches (5 cm) in diameter, twisting the ends nice and tight. Repeat with the other piece.

Place both logs in the oven, directly on the racks, and bake for 90 minutes. Remove and let cool, and then unwrap.

Slice into pieces about ½ inch (1.3 cm) thick and serve.

2 cups (288 g) vital wheat gluten flour
2 cups (240 g) whole wheat pastry flour
½ cup (60 g) nutritional yeast
1 tablespoon (6 g) ground black pepper
1 tablespoon (8 g) onion powder
1 tablespoon (8 g) garlic powder
1 tablespoon (7 g) paprika
1 tablespoon (8 g) cayenne pepper
1½ cups (355 ml) water
⅔ cup (160 ml) olive oil
⅔ cup (160 ml) tamari or soy sauce
⅓ cup (94 g) ketchup

**Yield: 20 sliders**

# 5

# BURGERS

A lot has changed in the world of veggie burgers. Tremendous progress has been made in commercially available veggie burgers — ones that are indistinguishable from their real-meat counterparts. Some of them even "bleed!" Controversy aside, no more do we have to suffer the hockey-puck-like frozen discs of funky-colored vegetable mash masquerading as a burger smelling faintly like a cross between cooked carrots and liquid smoke. That said, people still love to make their own veggie burgers from scratch, and this chapter gives you loads of recipes. **Quick tips:** Use your hands to knead the burger "dough" and a cookie cutter to shape the burgers.

# Sunday Afternoon Grillers

Just like their animal-based look-alikes, these burgers stand up to the best of them on a grill! Use these patties anywhere you want a meaty burger patty.

Preheat the oil in a flat-bottomed skillet over medium-high heat.

In a heat-safe bowl, pour boiling broth over the TVP granules, cover, and let sit for 10 minutes.

While the TVP is reconstituting, add the mushrooms, onion, and garlic to the pan. Sauté for 5 to 6 minutes, or until fragrant and beginning to brown.

In a food processor, combine the sautéed mushroom mixture, reconstituted TVP, gluten flour, nutritional yeast, tamari, and tomato paste. Process until well combined and "meaty" looking.

Transfer to a bowl and mix in the scallion. Form into 6 to 8 patties.

You can bake or fry these, but a great way to serve them is grilled. Use a lower flame, oil the grill, and slow cook them for about 10 minutes per side. BE PATIENT! Don't flip them too early or they will stick, and you won't get those sought-after grill marks.

These also freeze well, so you can make them in advance and bring them to your next outdoor get-together.

2 tablespoons (30 ml) vegetable oil

1 cup (235 ml) boiling vegetable broth or water

1 cup (96 g) TVP granules

8 ounces (227 g) mushrooms, roughly chopped

1 white onion, roughly chopped

2 cloves garlic, roughly chopped

1 cup (144 g) vital wheat gluten flour

¼ cup (30 g) nutritional yeast

¼ cup (60 ml) tamari or soy sauce

6 ounces (170 g) tomato paste

1 cup (96 g) diced scallion

**Yield: 6 to 8 patties**

**Note:** Oil the grill. Also rub a little oil on both sides of the burger before grilling; it will help you achieve those sought-after grill marks and help prevent sticking.

**Tip:** Replace the reconstituted TVP with 1¼ cups (232 g) prepared quinoa. When preparing your quinoa, use vegetable broth instead of water for extra flavor.

# All-American Burger

Here's a plain old burger that stands up to the grill with the best of its meaty cousins. Garnish as you would any burger. Add a slice of cheese for an All-American Cheeseburger.

2 tablespoons (28 ml) olive oil, plus
  more for frying (optional)
8 ounces (227 g) mushrooms, sliced
  or chopped
3 cloves garlic, minced
¾ cup (180 ml) vegetable broth
1 cup (96 g) TVP granules
¼ cup (30 g) nutritional yeast
½ cup (72 g) vital wheat gluten flour
1 tablespoon (8 g) ground mustard
1 tablespoon (8 g) onion powder
¼ teaspoon liquid smoke (optional)
Salt and pepper

**Yield: 4 burgers**

In a heavy-bottom skillet, heat the oil and sauté the mushrooms and garlic for 5 to 7 minutes, or until fragrant and beginning to brown.

Add the vegetable broth and bring to a simmer.

Add the TVP granules, mix well, cover, and remove from the heat. Let sit for 10 minutes.

When cool enough to handle, add the nutritional yeast, flour, ground mustard, onion powder, liquid smoke, and salt and pepper to taste and mix well using your hands.

Place in the fridge to cool for about 20 minutes. This will help the dough stiffen up a bit.

Form into 4 patties and cook as desired.

These are great grilled on the barbecue. If you use no foil, they stand up just fine. Cook them on a pretty hot spot on the grill for about 4 to 5 minutes on each side. Do rub a little extra oil on the patty before grilling to help prevent sticking.

They can also be fried in a skillet with a little oil for the same amount of time, or Air-Fried at 375°F (190°C) for 13 to 15 minutes.

# BLT and Avocado Burger

There is a ridiculous amount of imitation bacon bits in this recipe. Seriously, though, what's a BLT without a ton of bacon? Serve on a toasted sourdough bun with a schmear of mayo and, of course, a thick tomato slice and a nice leaf of crispy lettuce. Feel free to throw some bacon bits on top for good measure.

In a large bowl, combine the flours, bacon bits, garlic powder, onion powder, and pepper. In a separate bowl, mix together the tomatoes, oil, steak sauce, and ketchup. Add the wet ingredients to the dry and knead together until uniformly mixed. Let sit for 20 minutes.

Preheat the oven to 350°F (180°C, or gas mark 4). Line a baking sheet with parchment or a silicone baking mat.

Divide the mixture into 8 equal pieces, and flatten each piece. Place ½ avocado, mushed, into the center of 4 of the flattened pieces. Sandwich with the remaining 4 pieces and pinch the edges to seal.

Bake, covered in foil, for 20 minutes, then flip and bake for 15 minutes longer, or until firm.

1 cup (144 g) vital wheat gluten flour
1 cup (125 g) all-purpose flour
1 cup (80 g) imitation bacon bits, store-bought or homemade (page 176)
1 tablespoon (8 g) garlic powder
1 tablespoon (8 g) onion powder
½ teaspoon ground black pepper
1 cup (180 g) diced tomatoes
¼ cup (60 ml) vegetable oil
2 tablespoons (30 ml) steak sauce
2 tablespoons (30 g) ketchup
2 ripe avocados

**Yield: 4 huge burgers**

**Tip:** Make baked avocado fries to up the avocado goodness. Carefully slice a firm but ripe avocado into wedges. Coat with panko bread crumbs seasoned with salt, pepper, dried parsley, and garlic powder to taste. Bake at 425°F (220°C, or gas mark 7) for 5 to 7 minutes, or until the bread crumbs begin to brown. Serve with Chipotle Dipping Sauce (page 175).

# Basic Black Bean BBQ Burger

This hearty, meaty burger is a great burger to serve up to meat lovers. These taste great at a barbecue on a Soft White Bun (page 182) with a dollop of guacamole. Serve topped with a tangy slaw made with grated broccoli stems, chopped cilantro, and Yogurt Tahini Sauce (page 154), with some potatoes and corn on the cob on the side.

1 cup (96 g) TVP granules
1 scant cup (225 ml) water
½ cup (80 g) diced onion
1 can (15 ounces [425 g]) black beans, drained and rinsed
¾ cup (204 g) barbecue sauce, store-bought or homemade (page 155 or 166)
1 tablespoon (8 g) onion powder
1 tablespoon (8 g) garlic powder
1 teaspoon black pepper
3 tablespoons (48 g) peanut butter
½ cup (56 g) soy flour
Oil, for frying (optional)

**Yield: 8 burgers**

In a microwave-safe bowl, mix together the TVP granules and the water, cover tightly with plastic wrap, and microwave for 5 to 6 minutes. Alternatively, bring the water to a boil, pour over the TVP granules, cover, and let sit for 10 minutes.

When the TVP is cool enough to handle, mix in the onion, beans, barbecue sauce, onion powder, garlic powder, pepper, peanut butter, and flour. Using your hands, knead the dough to incorporate the ingredients fully, and until the TVP granules are no longer the consistency of granules. This will be about 5 minutes of hand manipulation. If your dough is too dry, add a bit of oil to the mix.

Refrigerate for at least 20 minutes.

Form into 8 patties and cook as desired. If baking, place on a baking sheet lined with parchment or a silicone baking mat and bake for 30 minutes at 350°F (180°C, or gas mark 4), loosely covered with a foil tent, flipping halfway through. If frying in oil, cook for 3 to 4 minutes per side, until a nice crispy golden crust forms. If using your Air-Fryer, set it at 375°F (190°C) for 16 to 18 minutes. These stand up well on the grill, too!

# Three Lentil Burger

While split peas aren't technically lentils, they are legumes—and they sure look like lentils. If you can't get red lentils, that's okay—just use all green. Influenced by Indian flavors found in Daal, this lentil burger is great served bunless topped with Yogurt Tahini Sauce (page 154) or Tzatziki Sauce (page 163).

¼ cup (48 g) dried red lentils
¼ cup (48 g) dried green lentils
¼ cup (56 g) dried split peas
1 pound (454 g) red potatoes, skin on, cut into chunks
2 tablespoons (28 ml) sesame oil
1 yellow onion, diced
4 cloves garlic, minced
1 teaspoon ground cumin
1 teaspoon coriander
1 teaspoon garam masala
¼ teaspoon turmeric
¼ to ½ cup (30 to 60 g) chickpea flour
Oil, for frying (optional)

**Yield: 8 burgers**

Fill a large pot with salted water and add the lentils and split peas. Bring to a boil. Boil for 15 minutes, then add the potatoes. Boil for 15 minutes longer, or until the potatoes are fork-tender.

Meanwhile, heat the oil in a skillet and sauté the onion and garlic until translucent, 5 to 7 minutes. Add the cumin, coriander, garam masala, and turmeric, stir to combine, and sauté for 2 or 3 more minutes.

After the lentils and potatoes are done, strain and return them to the pot. Add the onion and garlic mixture. With a potato masher, mash all the ingredients together. Let sit or refrigerate until cool, at least 20 minutes, or even overnight.

Preheat the oven to 350°F (180°C, or gas mark 4). Line a baking sheet with parchment or a silicone mat, or spray with cooking spray.

Add the flour to the mixture, starting with ¼ cup (30 g) and adding more if needed. Knead until the flour is well incorporated. Form into 8 patties and place on the prepared baking sheet. Bake for 15 minutes per side, covered in a foil tent, until firm and warmed all the way through. These can also be Air-Fried, at 395°F (201°C) for 14 to 16 minutes.

**Tip:** Wrap it up! On a flour tortilla, layer on a fragrant rice, a burger patty, halved, mixed greens, and Yogurt Tahini Sauce. Wrap it all up nice and tight and heat in a dry pan until browned. (For the rice, add 1 cup [180 g] basmati rice, 2 cups [470 ml] vegetable stock, and ¼ teaspoon each of cinnamon, ground cumin, and ground cardamom to a rice cooker. Once cooked, stir in ¼ cup [31 g] chopped pistachios [optional], ¼ cup [30 g] currants, and 2 tablespoons [30 ml] melted butter.)

# Korean BBQ Burger

Spicy with a hint of sweet, these burgers were inspired by some Korean spicy fries from a food truck in Long Beach, California—so good! If soy and wheat are not issues for you, serve these on a soft white bun, lightly toasted and schmeared with cream cheese mixed with a little bit of sriracha sauce. Add a little crunch by serving with a light and crisp cabbage slaw: Toss shredded green or purple cabbage with a bit of rice vinegar and season with red chili flakes to taste.

---

Add all the ingredients, except the oil, to a mixing bowl, and mash together using your hands. Really smoosh it together until there are almost no whole beans left in the mixture. Let rest for at least 20 minutes to thicken up a bit.

Form into 4 patties.

Panfry in oil over medium-high heat for 2 to 3 minutes per side, or until a golden, crispy crust is formed, or bake, uncovered, on a baking sheet lined with parchment or a silicone baking mat at 350°F (180°C, or gas mark 4) for 25 minutes, or until firm and just beginning to brown.

1 tablespoon (15 ml) sesame oil
1 to 3 tablespoons (15 to 45 g) chili garlic sauce or sambal oelek
4 cloves garlic, minced
1 cup (57 g) instant potato flakes
1 can (15 ounces [425 g]) white beans, drained and rinsed
2 tablespoons (12 g) finely chopped scallion or chives
½ cup (65 g) raw cashews, finely ground into a powder
2 tablespoons (42 g) agave nectar
2 tablespoons (16 g) cornstarch
3 tablespoons (45 ml) canola oil
Salt and pepper
Oil, for frying (optional)

**Yield: 4 burgers**

# Smoky BBQ Burgers

This is a meaty burger that won't fall apart. There's BBQ sauce inside the burger for moisture and flavor, and, of course, more BBQ sauce added on top of the burger. You could also make these into 6 to 8 slider-size burgers. Either way, serve 'em up with a side of fries ... and plenty of napkins.

These burgers can be panfried or oven-baked. If you are baking, preheat the oven to 350°F (180°C, or gas mark 4). Line a baking sheet with parchment paper and set aside.

Heat the olive oil in a small skillet over medium heat on the stove. Add the onion and garlic. Sauté for 5 to 6 minutes until soft and nearly all the liquid in the pan is gone. Turn off the heat.

In a food processor, pulse the walnuts until crumbly. Do not overprocess into flour; you want some small chunks for texture. Add the black beans, rice, sautéed onion and garlic, smoked paprika, salt, and pepper. Pulse just a few times until combined but still chunky.

Turn the mixture out into a large mixing bowl. Add the BBQ sauce and mix well with a spatula. Add the panko bread crumbs and mix well. You may need to get in there with your hands to mix and incorporate the bread crumbs evenly. The mixture should not be too sticky but should hold together well when pressed.

Divide the mixture in 4 sections. Form each section into a patty about 3 to 3½ inches (7.5 to 8.5 cm) in diameter.

If baking, place the patties on the prepared baking sheet. Bake for 15 minutes, gently flip over, and bake for 10 more minutes. Let sit for 5 minutes before serving.

If panfrying, spritz a skillet lightly with cooking spray and heat over medium heat. Place the patties in the pan with space in between each one. Cook for 10 to 15 minutes, gently flip over, and cook for another 10 to 15 minutes more. You may need to adjust the heat as you go if you find they are browning too quickly.

Serve on buns with more BBQ sauce and any toppings you desire.

2 teaspoons olive oil
½ cup (80 g) diced red onion (about ¼ large red onion)
1 clove garlic, minced
½ cup (50 g) raw walnuts
1 can (15 ounces, or 425 g) black beans, drained and rinsed (or 1½ cups [258 g] cooked beans)
1 cup (165 g) cooked rice (Leftover rice works great!)
1 teaspoon smoked paprika
¾ teaspoon fine salt
¼ teaspoon black pepper
¼ cup (60 ml) Sweet-and-Spicy BBQ Sauce (page 166) or store-bought BBQ sauce, plus more for topping
¾ cup (38 g) panko or (30 g) regular bread crumbs
4 burger buns
Lettuce, mayo, pickles, etc., for topping

**Yield: 4 burgers**

**Tip:** If you don't have a food processor, finely chop the walnuts with a sharp knife and mash the beans with a potato masher or fork. Mix everything together well in a mixing bowl.

# This Burger Is Nuts!

Protein-packed and full of earthy nutty flavor, this burger stands up well to many types of cuisine, so feel free to dress it up as you wish, or in other words … go nuts!

2 tablespoons (28 ml) olive oil, plus more for frying (optional)
8 ounces (227 g) mushrooms, sliced or chopped
3 cloves garlic, minced
¾ cup (180 ml) vegetable broth
1 cup (100 g) prepared brown rice
¼ cup (28 g) cashews, chopped
¼ cup (32 g) sunflower seeds
¼ cup (27 g) pecans, chopped
¼ cup (30 g) walnuts, chopped
¼ cup (30 g) nutritional yeast
½ cup (72 g) vital wheat gluten flour
1 tablespoon (8 g) ground mustard
1 tablespoon (8 g) onion powder
1 teaspoon liquid smoke (optional)
Salt and pepper, to taste

**Yield: 4 burgers (½ pound [227 g]) or 8 sliders (¼ pound [114 g])**

**Note:** To make this recipe gluten-free, substitute ½ cup (40 g) finely ground quick-cooking oats for the vital wheat gluten.

In a heavy-bottom skillet, heat the oil and sauté the mushrooms and garlic for 5 to 7 minutes, or until fragrant and beginning to brown. Add the vegetable broth and bring to a simmer. Add the rice, nuts, and seeds. Mix well, cover, and remove from the heat. Let sit for 10 minutes.

When cool enough to handle, add the nutritional yeast, gluten flour, ground mustard, onion powder, and liquid smoke, if using. Add salt and pepper to taste. Mix well using your hands.

Place in the fridge to cool for about 20 minutes. This will help the dough stiffen up a bit. Form into 4 to 8 patties, depending on size preference.

Preheat the oven to 350°F (180°C, or gas mark 4). Line a baking sheet with parchment, or a silicone baking mat. Arrange the patties on the mat, and bake for 25 minutes. Flip and bake an additional 15 minutes. Alternatively, you can panfry these burgers in a bit of oil for 4 to 5 minutes per side until crispy and golden.

# Tofu "Beef" or "Chicken" Patty

Super simple and flavorful, these perfectly round patties make a great substitute for the more labor-intensive beefy-type burgers earlier in this chapter and for any fuss-free simple "chicken" sandwiches.

Carefully cut the block of tofu into slabs about ¼-inch (6 mm) thick. Using a 4-inch (10 cm) cookie cutter, cut 4 rounds from the slabs. Set aside.

Add the remaining ingredients to a resealable bag, or shallow dish with a lid, and mix well. Add the tofu rounds to the mixture and marinate for at least 30 minutes, or up to overnight.

Cook as desired. This patty can be baked at 350°F (176°C) for 10 minutes per side, Air-Fried for 12 to 14 minutes at 375°F (190°C), or panfried in a nonstick pan over medium-high heat for about 3 minutes per side, or until warmed all the way through.

**Tip:** Freezing tofu before using it in recipes transforms the texture. Cut your tofu into rounds, arrange on a baking sheet in a single layer, and freeze. Thaw and gently press out any excess moisture before placing into the marinade. They'll suck up that marinade like a sponge and, once cooked, you'll really taste the chewier texture and added flavor.

1 pound (454 g) super- or extra-firm tofu, drained and pressed (see Note)

**FOR BEEF:**
½ cup (120 ml) water
½ cup (120 ml) soy sauce or tamari
¼ cup (60 ml) steak sauce
2 tablespoons (16 g) garlic powder
2 tablespoons (16 g) onion powder
½ teaspoon pepper

**FOR CHICKEN:**
1 cup (235 ml) water or low-sodium vegetable broth
3 tablespoons (23 g) nutritional yeast
1 tablespoon (2 g) dried parsley
1 tablespoon (8 g) onion powder
1½ teaspoons garlic powder
1 teaspoon celery seed
½ teaspoon salt
½ teaspoon dried oregano
½ teaspoon turmeric
¼ teaspoon thyme
¼ teaspoon dried rosemary
¼ teaspoon black pepper

**Yield: 4 burgers**

**Note:** A tip for pressing tofu: After you've drained the excess liquid from the package, place the block sandwiched between two folded dish towels. Place a heavy book or pan on top to gently press the moisture out and let sit for 30 minutes to 1 hour to completely press.

# Pintos and Rice Burger

This one couldn't be simpler. Simply mush all the ingredients together and bake or fry. While these do taste a tad better fried, the baked version tastes delicious too—and is certainly better for the waistline.

1 can (15 ounces [425 g]) pinto beans, drained
2 cups (330 g) cooked brown or white rice
1 cup (180 g) diced tomatoes
1 cup (160 g) diced onion
½ cup (70 g) yellow cornmeal
½ cup (62 g) all-purpose flour
1 jalapeño pepper, seeded if desired, and diced
1 tablespoon (15 g) minced garlic
1 teaspoon hot sauce
½ teaspoon ground cumin
Salt and pepper
Oil, for frying (optional)

**Yield: 8 burgers**

**Note:** Enjoy this one a couple of ways: as a burger on a toasted bun smothered with guacamole and topped with a few slices of jalapeños; served up with a big old side of chips and salsa or a grilled ear of corn on the cob (as shown here); or sandwiched in a flour tortilla and grilled quesadilla style, with some Nacho Cheesy Sauce (page 154), guacamole, and sour cream.

In a mixing bowl, combine all the ingredients except the oil and knead with your hands.

Form into 8 patties and cook as desired.

Panfry in plenty of oil for 4 to 5 minutes per side, until golden and crispy; Air-Fry at 375°F (190°C) for 16 to 18 minutes; or bake, uncovered, at 350°F (180°C, or gas mark 4) for 15 minutes on a baking sheet lined with parchment or a silicone baking mat, and then flip and bake for 15 minutes longer, until firm and just beginning to brown.

# South by Southwest Burger

This recipe yields eight whoppin' burgers, so unless you plan on feeding lots of hungry veganos, feel free to cut the recipe in half, or freeze the patties for quick dinners throughout the week. Serve on a nice hearty bun with a schmear of sour cream and some salsa or serve with tortilla chips and Cilantro Lime Rice (page 148).

1 cup (96 g) TVP granules
1 cup (235 ml) vegetable broth or water
1 can (15 ounces [425 g]) black beans, drained
2 cups (280 g) canned, fresh, or frozen corn kernels
2 cups (330 g) cooked brown rice
1 heaping cup (190 g) diced tomatoes, drained
½ cup (80 g) finely diced onion
¼ cup (40 g) finely diced jarred jalapeños (optional)
3 tablespoons (45 ml) canola oil
1 cup (144 g) vital wheat gluten flour
¼ cup (32 g) cornstarch
2 tablespoons (16 g) garlic powder
2 tablespoons (16 g) onion powder
1 teaspoon unsweetened cocoa powder
1 teaspoon paprika
Salt and pepper

**Yield: 8 burgers**

**Note:** Serve these up torta style by using bolillo or telera rolls in place of buns. Spread one side of the roll with a thick layer of guacamole, and the other with sour cream. Add the patty and shredded lettuce. Garnish with pico de gallo.

In a microwave-safe bowl, mix together the TVP granules and broth, cover tightly with plastic wrap, and microwave for 5 to 6 minutes. Alternatively, bring the broth to a boil, pour over the TVP granules, cover, and let sit for 10 minutes. Let cool.

In a mixing bowl, combine the beans, corn, cooked rice, tomatoes, onion, jalapeños, and oil. In a separate bowl, mix together the flour, cornstarch, garlic powder, onion powder, cocoa, paprika, and salt and pepper to taste.

When cool enough to handle, combine the reconstituted TVP with the rice and veggie mixture. Mix well with your hands so that the beans and rice start to get mushed in pretty well with the TVP. Add the flour and spice mixture, and knead for a few minutes until a nice dough forms. Place the mixture in the refrigerator for at least 30 minutes to rest.

Preheat the oven to 350°F (180°C, or gas mark 4). Line a baking sheet with parchment or a silicone baking mat.

Form into 8 patties, place on the prepared baking sheet, and bake, uncovered, for 15 minutes, then flip and bake for 15 minutes longer, until firm and just beginning to brown.

# Couscous Pantry Burger

If you've ever set out to go a month without buying any food, using only what you already had in your kitchen, you can appreciate why these are called pantry burgers. They're good topped with a slice of mozzarella or some roasted garlic or Aioli Dipping Sauce (page 159). A bit of Quick and Easy Marinara Sauce (page 166) would be tasty, too. Fried Zucchini (page 144) would be a perfect side dish. The ideal bun? Try the Rustica Bun on page 183.

Bring the vegetable broth and tomato sauce to a boil. Lower the heat to a simmer.

Add the couscous and TVP, stir well, cover, and remove from the heat. Let sit for 10 minutes to absorb all of the liquid.

When cool enough to handle, add the basil, garlic, zucchini, flaxseed mixture, flour, nutritional yeast, and 2 tablespoons (30 ml) oil. Mix together and knead so that all ingredients are well incorporated and a nice patty-able consistency is reached.

Form into 8 patties and fry in oil for 3 to 5 minutes per side, until golden and crispy. Baking or Air-Frying these is not recommended because they will get too dried out.

2 cups (470 ml) vegetable broth
1 can (14 ounces [392 g]) tomato sauce
1 cup (174 g) dry couscous
1 cup (96 g) TVP granules
1 tablespoon (2 g) dried basil or 3 tablespoons (9 g) fresh, finely chopped
2 tablespoons (30 g) minced garlic
¼ cup (31 g) shredded or grated zucchini
2 tablespoons (19 g) ground flaxseed mixed with 3 tablespoons (45 ml) warm water
1 cup (120 g) whole wheat pastry flour
¼ cup (30 g) nutritional yeast
2 tablespoons (28 ml) olive oil, plus extra for frying

**Yield: 8 burgers**

# Super Quinoa Burger

Since quinoa is the super grain, these are dubbed Super Burgers! This one really tastes good on lettuce, such as red leaf. A nice big leaf, topped with the patty, some alfalfa sprouts, and drizzled with Yogurt Tahini Sauce (page 154 and pictured here). So yum, but feel free to make your bun dreams come true, too. Brown rice makes a good side dish.

Bring the vegetable broth to a boil.

Meanwhile, in a dry pan, heat the uncooked quinoa until it begins to pop (this will happen fairly quickly).

Add the quinoa to the broth, and lower the heat to medium. Cover and cook for 12 minutes, or until all of the broth is absorbed. Remove from the heat, fluff with a fork, and let sit, uncovered, to cool.

In a large mixing bowl, combine the beans, peas, cashew powder, curry, ginger, tahini, and sesame oil. Gently mush the peas and beans, but don't completely mash; chunky is good.

When the quinoa is cooled, fold it into the mixture and add the cornstarch and salt and pepper to taste. Mix well using your hands.

Refrigerate for at least 20 minutes to thicken up a bit before forming into 8 patties.

Panfry in a smidge of oil in a pan until golden on each side, about 3 minutes per side. These taste best panfried. The oven makes them too dry, and they won't hold up well on a grill.

1½ cups (355 ml) vegetable broth
1 cup (173 g) uncooked quinoa
1 can (15 ounces [425 g]) cannellini or navy beans, rinsed and drained
2 cups (300 g) fresh or frozen green peas
½ cup (65 g) raw cashews, ground into a fine powder
1 teaspoon green curry paste
1 teaspoon ground ginger
2 tablespoons (32 g) tahini paste
2 tablespoons (28 ml) sesame oil
½ cup (64 g) cornstarch
Salt and pepper
Oil, for frying

**Yield: 8 burgers**

**Tip:** These have a wonderful flavor. In fact, they wouldn't make a bad side dish just as is. Plop a scoop on a plate next to a main dish and done.

# Pepperoni Pizza Burger

Pepperoni pizza as a burger? Whhaaaat? For extra pizza goodness, place some shredded mozzarella on the top of your burger during the last few minutes of cooking to get it all nice and melty. For a bun? Try garlic naan or 50/50 Flatbread (page 183), and pictured here), schmeared with Simple Pesto (page 156, and pictured here).

1 tablespoon (8 g) freshly ground black pepper
1 tablespoon (7 g) paprika
1 teaspoon whole aniseed
1 teaspoon salt
1 teaspoon red pepper flakes
1 teaspoon sugar
1 teaspoon dried basil
1 teaspoon chipotle powder or cayenne pepper
1 tablespoon (8 g) garlic powder
1 cup (96 g) TVP granules
1 cup (235 ml) water
2 tablespoons (30 ml) liquid smoke
2 tablespoons (30 ml), plus ¼ cup (60 ml) olive oil, divided
6 ounces (170 g) tomato paste
1 cup (144 g) vital wheat gluten flour
⅓ cup (80 g) sour cream, store-bought or homemade nondairy (page 162)
Oil, for frying (optional)

**Yield: 6 burgers**

In a microwave-safe dish, combine the pepper, paprika, aniseed, salt, red pepper flakes, sugar, basil, chipotle powder, garlic powder, TVP, water, liquid smoke, and 2 tablespoons (30 ml) olive oil. Cover tightly with plastic wrap and microwave on high for 5 to 6 minutes. Alternatively, bring the water to a boil and pour over the TVP mixed with the spices, oil, and liquid smoke, cover, and let sit for 10 minutes. Let cool.

Add the tomato paste, flour, remaining ¼ cup (60 ml) oil, and sour cream to the cooled TVP mixture. Using your hands, mash everything together and form into 6 patties.

You can panfry, Air-Fry, or bake these with great results. Panfry in just a smidge of oil for 5 minutes per side over medium-high heat, or until a nice crispy crust forms. Air-Fry at 375°F (190°C) for 16 to 18 minutes. Or bake them at 350°F (180°C, or gas mark 4) on a baking sheet lined with parchment or a silicone baking mat, uncovered, for 30 minutes, flipping halfway through.

**Tip:** Make the ultimate pizza pockets using premade pizza dough! Preheat your oven to 425°F (220°C, or gas mark 7). Line a baking sheet with parchment. Divide the dough into 6 pieces, and roll out thin on a well-floured surface. Place a dollop of Quick and Easy Marinara Sauce (page 166) or Simple Pesto (page 156) on one half of the dough, add a Pepperoni Pizza Burger on top of the sauce, and place a handful of mozzarella shreds on top. Fold the other half of the dough over and seal the edges with the tines of a fork. Slice 2 to 3 vent holes in the top with a sharp knife. Brush lightly with melted butter and sprinkle with a pinch of dried basil and paprika. Bake for 12 to 15 minutes, or until the crust is golden.

# Tabbouleh Burger

Tabbouleh has a clean, light flavor that just tastes healthy. If you have a food processor, now is the time to use it.

**To make the tabbouleh salad:** Bring the water, lightly salted, to a boil. Add the bulgur wheat, lower the heat to a simmer, and cook, uncovered, for about 10 minutes, or until all the liquid is absorbed. Set aside to cool.

In a large bowl, combine the parsley, cucumber, tomatoes, mint, olive oil, garlic, lemon juice, and salt and pepper to taste. Add the cooled bulgur and mix thoroughly.

Stop here and you have a perfectly good tabbouleh salad. You don't have to make it into burgers.

**To make the burgers:** Preheat the oven to 350°F (180°C, or gas mark 4). Line a baking pan with parchment or a silicone baking mat.

Add the flour and cornstarch to the Tabbouleh Salad mixture. Knead until well incorporated. If your mixture is too wet, add a little more flour. Form into 10 patties. Bake for 40 to 45 minutes, flipping halfway through, until firm and just beginning to brown. You can eat them just like this, but they get extra yummy if you panfry them in a little sesame oil after you bake them, just to get a little golden crispy crust! Alternatively, use your Air-Fryer at 375°F (190°C) for 18 to 20 minutes.

FOR TABBOULEH SALAD:
3 cups (705 ml) water
1 cup (176 g) uncooked bulgur wheat
3 cups (180 g) finely chopped
    fresh parsley
1 large cucumber, seeded and diced
    (about 2 cups [270 g])
1 cup (180 g) diced tomatoes (approx.
    2 seeded tomatoes)
¼ cup (12 g) finely chopped mint leaves
½ cup (120 ml) olive oil
3 tablespoons (45 g) minced garlic
3 tablespoons (45 ml) lemon juice
Salt and pepper

FOR BURGERS:
1 recipe Tabbouleh Salad
1 cup (120 g) whole wheat flour
3 tablespoons (24 g) cornstarch
2 tablespoons (30 ml) sesame oil
    (optional)

**Yield: 10 burgers**

**Note:** Because these taste great warm or cold, make them into little slider appetizers to bring along to your next potluck. Make 20 burger patties and reduce the cook time by 10 minutes (3 to 4 minutes less in the Air-Fryer). Start with slider-size 50/50 Flatbreads (page 183). Add a bit of hummus, a few leaves of baby spinach, a slice of Roma tomato, and a dollop of Tzatziki Sauce (page 163.

# The Better Mac

Here you go, Micky Dees, the song's been fixed for you! "Two all vegan patties, Better Sauce, lettuce, cheeze, pickles, onions, on a sesame seed bun!" Ahh, the Big Mac. A shimmering icon of the good ol' US of A. Excess at its finest. (I'm talking to you, extra bun in the middle.)

**FOR BETTER SAUCE:**

½ cup (112 g) mayo, store-bought or homemade vegan (page 161)

2 tablespoons (34 g) ketchup

2 tablespoons (30 g) dill or sweet pickle relish

1 teaspoon stone ground or whole grain mustard

1 teaspoon minced garlic

½ teaspoon onion powder

½ teaspoon dried dill (or 1½ teaspoons fresh)

Salt and pepper, to taste

**FOR BURGERS:**

4 sesame seed buns

Vegan butter (optional)

½ cup Better Sauce, prepared

1 cup (72 g) shredded iceberg lettuce

½ cup (80 g) finely diced white onion

4 beefy-type burger patties, such as the All-American Burger (page 72), prepared

2 slices of your favorite American-style vegan cheese

10 slices of dill pickle

**Yield: 2 burgers and just over ½ cup (135 ml) sauce**

**To make the Better Sauce:** Whisk all the ingredients together until well combined. Store in the refrigerator in an airtight container for up to a week, until ready to use.

**To make the burgers:** Separate the buns, set aside or discard two top buns, leaving you with two tops and four bottoms. Lightly butter each bun, if desired, and toast in a dry skillet until lightly browned.

Spread all the buns with a thick layer of Better Sauce.

Pile shredded lettuce evenly on all four bun bottoms.

Sprinkle diced onion evenly on top of all of the lettuce shreds.

Place a burger patty on two of the burger bottoms.

Place a slice of cheese on each of the two burgers.

Place the remaining two bun bottoms on top of the cheese, lettuce side up.

Place the remaining burger patties on top.

Top the burger patties with five slices of pickle each.

Complete the burger with the two remaining top buns and serve.

**Tip:** Replace the shredded iceberg lettuce with shredded dino lacinato (dinosaur) kale and replace the Better Sauce with Creamy Sesame Sriracha Sauce (page 164). If you're looking for an oil-free version of the sauce, replace the vegan mayo with silken tofu.

# Double Up

Out in California they have In-N-Out Burger with its iconic crisscrossed palm trees in front of every restaurant, and bible verses on the bottom of every cup. They have an almost cult-like following with secret menu items (including a vegan option!). Die-hard fans, who, once they move out of Cali, complain of In-N-Out withdrawal. Their signature sandwich is a Double-Double, but this version's mustard-grilled burgers and two sauces really take it over the top. Serve it up with a side of fries topped with more Cheezy Sauce, chopped grilled onions, and a generous pour-over of Better Sauce.

**To make the mustard-grilled patties:** Follow the burger recipe as directed up until the cooking instructions. To cook, heat the oil in a frying pan or skillet over medium-high heat. Prior to adding the patties to the pan, coat each patty with 1 tablespoon (15 ml) of yellow mustard using your hands. Add to the pan and fry for 4 to 5 minutes per side.

**To make the grilled onions:** Reduce the heat to medium-low. Add the oil to the pan to preheat. Add the onions and salt, and toss to coat. Cook, tossing and stirring every so often until the onions are translucent and browned, about 15 minutes. Once the onions begin to look dry, add 1 tablespoon (15 ml) water to the pan and stir. Continue cooking until the water evaporates and the onions start sizzling again. Repeat, adding 1 tablespoon (15 ml) of water each time until the onions are dark brown and super soft, about three times total.

**To assemble the burgers:** Slather Better Sauce onto the bottom bun and layer on the pickles, tomato, and lettuce, and 1 Mustard-Grilled Patty.

In a small bowl, mix together the Cheezy Sauce and grilled onions. Place half of the cheezy onion mixture on top of the patty, then add the second patty and pour the remaining cheezy onion mixture on top. Finish with the top bun and serve immediately.

**FOR MUSTARD-GRILLED PATTIES:**
½ recipe All-American Burgers (page 72) prepared as directed at left
2 tablespoons (34 g) yellow mustard
Oil, for frying

**FOR GRILLED ONIONS:**
1 tablespoon (15 ml) mild-flavored vegetable oil
1 large white or yellow onion, diced
½ teaspoon salt
Water, as needed

**FOR EACH BURGER:**
2 tablespoons (30 ml) Better Sauce (page 92)
1 soft white bun, store-bought or homemade (page 182), toasted
4 slices of dill pickle
1 slice of tomato
1 leaf romaine or green leaf lettuce
2 Mustard-Grilled Patties
¼ cup (60 ml) Cheezy Sauce (page 67)
1 recipe Grilled Onions

**Yield: 2 burgers**

# Sun-Dried Tomato and Pesto Burger

This one is good on two crusty pieces of bread schmeared with extra pesto, grilled like a panini, and a few fresh leaves of spinach.

1 tablespoon (15 ml) olive oil, plus more
    for frying (optional)
8 ounces (227 g) mushrooms, sliced
    or chopped
1 white or yellow onion, chopped
¼ cup (28 g) sun-dried tomato pieces,
    packed in oil, drained (see Note)
2 cups (330 g) cooked brown rice
1 recipe Simple Pesto (page 156)
Salt and pepper
½ to 1 cup (80 to 160 g) brown rice flour

**Yield: 8 burgers**

**Note:** Have you ever made your own sun-dried tomatoes? It's very simple, but it does take a long time ... and doesn't require any sun! Simply wash and halve tomatoes and gently rinse out the seeds. Place on a cookie sheet lined with parchment or a silicone mat, and bake at 200°F (95°C) until dry to the touch, and leathery in texture, but still pliable. This could take 8 to 10 hours (or more). When ready, cool before storing in an airtight container in the refrigerator.

In a skillet, heat the 1 tablespoon (15 ml) of olive oil and sauté the mushrooms and onion over medium-high heat for 7 to 10 minutes, or until fragrant, translucent, and reduced by half. Add the sautéed onion and mushrooms, tomato pieces, rice, pesto, and salt and pepper to taste to a food processor and pulse until well combined but still a little chunky. Transfer to a mixing bowl.

Depending on the moisture content of your mixture, knead in the flour a little at a time until a good consistency for forming patties is reached. Refrigerate for at least 20 minutes, so the flour can absorb the flavors and moisture of the mixture. Form into 8 patties and cook as desired.

If baking, use a baking sheet lined with parchment or a silicone baking mat, and bake at 350°F (180°C, or gas mark 4) for 15 minutes, and then flip and bake for 15 minutes longer, until firm and just beginning to brown. If frying, make sure there is enough oil in the pan to prevent it from sticking and fry over medium-high heat for 4 to 5 minutes per side, or until a nice golden crust forms.

*6*

# BOUNTIFUL BOWLS FOR THE ENTIRE DAY

You might know them as power bowls, bliss bowls, nourish bowls, or hippie bowls, but no matter what name they go by, Buddha bowls are a one-bowl meal packed with nourishing, real-food ingredients. Each bowl starts with a base typically made up of whole grains, rice, noodles, or legumes. Then it gets loaded with cooked or raw vegetables, often a handful or two of fresh greens, and a boost of protein before getting finished off with a dressing, sauce, or broth. Bowls are ideal for picky eaters who want to customize their own, as most components are kept separate until added to individual bowls.

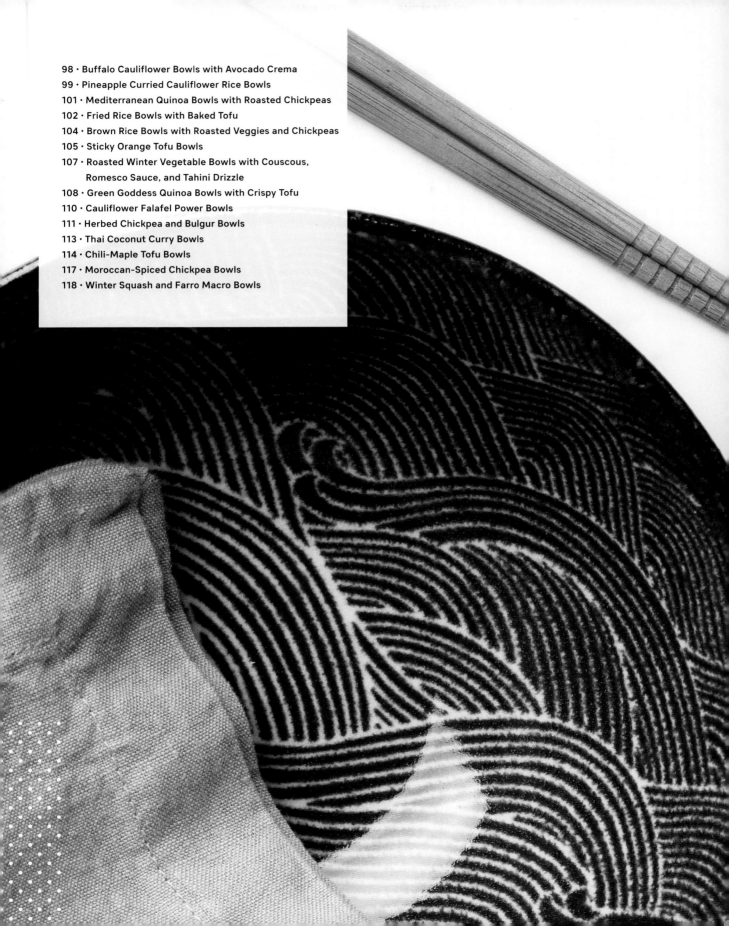

# Buffalo Cauliflower Bowls with Avocado Crema

Who doesn't love buffalo sauce? It's spicy and tangy and so delicious! If you're worried about the heat, the so-good-you'll-want-to-eat-it-by-the-spoonful Avocado Crema is going to help to cool things down.

**FOR BUFFALO CAULIFLOWER:**
1 head cauliflower, cut into florets
   (about 4-5 cups [500-600 g])
1 tablespoon (15 ml) olive oil
1 teaspoon salt
¼ teaspoon garlic powder
¼ teaspoon black pepper
½ cup (120 ml) buffalo-style hot sauce

**FOR AVOCADO CREMA:**
1 avocado, peel and pit removed
1 container (5.5 ounces, or 155 g)
   plain yogurt
Juice of ½ lime
½ teaspoon salt, or to taste

**FOR BOWLS:**
2 cups (370 g) cooked quinoa
4 cups (400 g) coleslaw mix
¼ cup (4 g) chopped cilantro

**Yield: 4 servings**

Preheat the oven to 450°F (230°C, or gas mark 8). Lightly spray a rimmed baking sheet with cooking spray and set aside.

**For the Buffalo Cauliflower:** In a large mixing bowl, combine the cauliflower florets, olive oil, salt, garlic powder, and pepper. Mix well to coat evenly. Spread the cauliflower out onto the prepared baking sheet in one even layer. Try to leave a little room between the florets if possible. Roast for 15 minutes.

Pour the buffalo hot sauce into the same mixing bowl you used before. Add the roasted cauliflower and mix well to evenly coat. Spread out onto the baking sheet again in one even layer and roast for another 5 to 10 minutes until just tender.

**For the Avocado Crema:** Add all the ingredients to a blender or food processor and purée until smooth.

**To build your bowls:** Add ½ cup (92 g) of quinoa to each bowl with 1 cup (100 g) of coleslaw mix, one-quarter of the roasted buffalo cauliflower, 1 tablespoon (1 g) of cilantro, and a few tablespoons (around 45 g) of Avocado Crema.

**Tip:** If you aren't keen on spicy, only coat half of the cauliflower in the buffalo sauce and shake off any excess before returning it to the baking sheet.

# Pineapple Curried Cauliflower Rice Bowls

If you're cutting back on grains, then this one is for you. Shredded cauliflower brilliantly stands in for rice in this dish. Bright, sweet pineapple balances the earthiness of the curry perfectly. Use canned pineapple here for convenience all year long, but feel free to use fresh if it's in season.

**For the Chickpeas:** Preheat the oven to 400°F (200°C, or gas mark 6).

Toss the chickpeas with olive oil, salt, and pepper and spread out onto a rimmed baking sheet in one even layer. Bake for 25 to 30 minutes, shaking the pan every 10 minutes to toss the chickpeas. Set aside. The chickpeas will continue to crisp up while they sit.

**For the Curried Cauliflower Rice:** Working in 2 to 3 batches, pulse the cauliflower in a food processor, stopping to scrape down the sides as necessary, until the texture resembles rice. Do not overprocess! You should have about 4 cups (400 g) of riced cauliflower. Set aside.

Heat the coconut oil in a large pan over medium heat on the stove. Add the onion and sauté for 5 to 6 minutes until soft and translucent. Add the bell pepper and carrots and sauté for 5 to 6 minutes until starting to soften. Add the curry powder, garlic powder, and salt and sauté for 1 minute until fragrant. Add the riced cauliflower and sauté for 7 to 8 minutes, stirring occasionally to prevent sticking. Add the green peas and pineapple chunks, stir to combine, and sauté for 2 to 3 minutes to heat through.

**To assemble the bowls:** Divide the mixture among 4 bowls and top with one-quarter of the roasted chickpeas. Sprinkle with 1 tablespoon (about 9 g) of pumpkin seeds and 1 tablespoon (1 g) of cilantro.

**FOR CHICKPEAS:**
1 can (15 ounces, or 425 g) chickpeas, drained and rinsed
1 teaspoon olive oil
Salt and black pepper

**FOR CURRIED CAULIFLOWER RICE:**
1 head cauliflower, broken into florets
1 tablespoon (14 g) coconut oil or (15 ml) olive oil
1 yellow onion, diced
1 red bell pepper, seeded and diced
1 cup (110 g) shredded carrots
2 teaspoons yellow curry powder
1 teaspoon garlic powder
¾ teaspoon salt
1 cup (130 g) frozen green peas
1 can (20 ounces, or 560 g) pineapple chunks, drained

**FOR SERVING:**
¼ cup (35 g) raw shelled pumpkin seeds
¼ cup (4 g) chopped cilantro

**Yield: 4 servings**

# Mediterranean Quinoa Bowls with Roasted Chickpeas

These bowls just might make you feel healthier simply by looking at them: superfood quinoa, protein-packed chickpeas, nutritional powerhouse greens, and vibrantly fresh cucumber-tomato salad. The Citrus Tahini Sauce is the perfect creamy sauce to bring it all together.

**For the Roasted Chickpeas:** Preheat the oven to 400°F (200°C, or gas mark 6). Line a rimmed baking sheet with parchment paper and set aside.

Toss the chickpeas in a bowl with the spices and olive oil; mix well. Spread them out onto the prepared baking sheet in an even layer. Roast for 15 minutes, stir the chickpeas, and roast for 10 to 15 more minutes until browning and crunchy. They will continue to crisp up as they cool.

**For the Quinoa:** Heat the oil in a pot over medium heat on the stove. Add the quinoa and sauté for 2 to 3 minutes to toast, stirring frequently to prevent burning. Carefully add the vegetable broth. Increase the heat to high and bring to a boil, cover, and then reduce the heat to low. Simmer for 10 to 15 minutes until tender. Add salt and pepper, if desired, to taste.

While the quinoa is cooking, toss the cucumbers, tomatoes, onion, parsley, lemon, and salt in a bowl. Mix well. Taste and adjust the seasoning, if needed.

**To assemble the bowls:** Place 1 cup (55 g) of salad greens in the bottom of a bowl. Top it with ¾ cup (139 g) of quinoa, one-quarter of the cucumber-tomato salad, one-quarter of the roasted chickpeas, and 2 to 3 tablespoons (28 to 45 ml) of the Citrus Tahini Sauce.

**FOR ROASTED CHICKPEAS:**

1 can (15 ounces, or 425 g) chickpeas, drained, rinsed, and patted dry
1 teaspoon ground cumin
½ teaspoon dried oregano
¼ teaspoon ground turmeric
¼ teaspoon garlic powder
¼ teaspoon salt
1 teaspoon olive oil

**FOR QUINOA:**

1 tablespoon (15 ml) olive oil
1 cup (173 g) dry quinoa, rinsed well with cold water
1½ cups (355 ml) low-sodium vegetable broth
Salt and black pepper

**FOR BOWLS:**

1 English cucumber, diced
1 pint (275 g) grape tomatoes, halved
¼ red onion, diced
3-4 tablespoons (12–15 g) chopped fresh parsley
Juice of 1 lemon
¼–½ teaspoon salt, or to taste
4 cups (220 g) baby salad greens
1 recipe Citrus Tahini Sauce (page 174)

**Yield: 4 servings**

# Fried Rice Bowls with Baked Tofu

Throw away your carry-out menus and make this easy homemade fried rice bowl instead. It's so much healthier than restaurant versions, but just as satisfying.

3 tablespoons (45 ml) tamari, coconut aminos, or soy sauce

¼ cup (63 g) hoisin sauce (see Note)

3 tablespoons (45 ml) rice wine vinegar

3 cloves garlic, minced

2 teaspoons ground ginger

A few shakes of sriracha (optional)

1 tablespoon (15 ml) peanut oil

1 cup (90 g) chopped cabbage

½ red bell pepper, seeded and diced

1 cup (63 g) snow peas, halved

3 scallions, diced

½ cup (65 g) sweet green peas

4 cups (780 g) leftover cooked brown rice

1 recipe Addictive Tofu (page 180), either version

1–2 teaspoons sesame oil (optional)

2–3 tablespoons (16–24 g) white sesame seeds

**Yield: 6 servings**

**Note:** Hoisin sauce is an Asian barbecue sauce. It's thick and savory with a hint of sweet and spicy. It brings so much flavor with very little effort. You can usually find hoisin sauce near the Asian noodles and soy sauces in your grocery store.

Whisk together the tamari, hoisin, rice wine vinegar, garlic, ginger, and sriracha, if using, in a small bowl or measuring cup and set aside.

Heat the peanut oil in a skillet over medium-high heat, add the cabbage, bell pepper, and snow peas. Cook for 2 to 3 minutes, stirring frequently, until just starting to soften. You want the veggies to retain their fresh flavor and still give a nice crunch, so don't overcook!

Add the scallions and sweet peas and cook for 1 minute while stirring. Add the sauce to the veggies and stir to coat. Add the rice and stir until evenly coated in the sauce. Continue cooking for 3 to 4 minutes to heat through.

To serve, divide the fried rice among 6 bowls. Top with Addictive Tofu and a few more dashes of sriracha if you like the heat. Drizzle with sesame oil, if using, and sprinkle with sesame seeds.

**Tip:** This dish is easy to customize. Use green beans instead of snow peas or shredded carrots instead of bell peppers. Or add those extra veggies in addition to the others. If you increase the amount of vegetables used, decrease the amount of rice to ensure there is enough sauce to coat the dish.

# Brown Rice Bowls with Roasted Veggies and Chickpeas

This is a classic grains, veggies, protein, and sauce bowl. It's all your favorites in one bowl drizzled with the most amazing sweet tahini sauce. The whole thing comes together quickly and easily, and everyone will clean their plates.

**FOR VEGETABLES AND CHICKPEAS:**
1 cup (190 g) brown rice (Quick-cook is fine!)
1 head cauliflower, cut into bite-size florets
1 head broccoli, cut into bite-size florets
1 can (15 ounces, or 425 g) chickpeas (or 1½ cups [246 g] cooked chickpeas)
3 medium carrots, cut into coins
2 teaspoons olive oil
Salt and black pepper
2 tablespoons (16 g) sesame seeds

**FOR CREAMY SWEET TAHINI DRESSING:**
¼ cup (60 g) tahini
3 tablespoons (45 ml) balsamic vinegar
2 tablespoons (40 g) pure maple syrup
1 clove garlic, minced
3 tablespoons (12 g) nutritional yeast
¼ cup (60 ml) water, plus more as needed to thin
Salt and black pepper

**Yield: 4 servings**

Preheat the oven to 400°F (200°C, or gas mark 6). Line 2 rimmed baking sheets with parchment paper and set aside.

Cook the rice according to package directions.

Spread the cauliflower and broccoli on one baking sheet. Spread the chickpeas and carrots on another baking sheet. Drizzle 1 teaspoon of olive oil over each baking sheet and give the veggies a toss. Sprinkle with salt and pepper.

Roast for 20 to 30 minutes, turning the pans and giving them a shake every 10 minutes. The cauliflower and broccoli take about 30 minutes and the carrots and chickpeas take about 20, so start the broccoli/cauliflower first and put the chickpeas/carrots in after the first 10 minutes. Every oven is different, so keep an eye on everything to make sure you don't burn them.

**For the Creamy Sweet Tahini Dressing:** Combine all the ingredients in a small bowl or cup and whisk until smooth. Add more water to thin, as needed. Taste and adjust the seasoning. Set aside.

When the veggies and chickpeas are done, make your bowls! Add a little rice, broccoli, cauliflower, carrots, chickpeas, sesame seeds, and Creamy Sweet Tahini Dressing in each individual bowl.

# Sticky Orange Tofu Bowls

This dish will remind you of your favorite take-out, but it's much healthier as you control the ingredients. The sticky sweet orange sauce is loaded with diced peppers, and it's ready in under thirty minutes. Roasted cauliflower makes a great addition to this dish or as a replacement for the Addictive Tofu.

Make the Addictive Tofu and set aside.

Wipe down the same skillet, add the olive oil, and heat on the stove over medium heat. Add the onion and sauté for 5 to 6 minutes until soft and translucent. Add the garlic and bell peppers and sauté for 5 to 6 minutes until they start to soften.

Add the orange juice, tamari, maple syrup, and rice vinegar to the skillet and stir to combine.

In a small bowl, whisk the cornstarch and water until smooth. Add it to the skillet, increase the heat to high to bring to a boil, and then reduce the heat to medium-low. Simmer for 15 to 20 minutes until thick and glossy.

Divide the rice among 4 bowls. Pour ¾ cup (175 ml) of the sauce over the rice and one-quarter of the Addictive Tofu on top. Garnish with scallions and a sprinkle of sesame seeds.

**Tip:** The tofu can be made ahead of time and kept in the fridge for 2 to 3 days until ready to use. It can also be added to the sauce before serving if you prefer.

1 recipe Addictive Tofu (page 180), either version
1 tablespoon (15 ml) olive oil
½ red onion, diced
3 cloves garlic, minced
2 sweet bell peppers, seeded and diced
1½ cups (355 ml) fresh orange juice
¼ cup (60 ml) tamari, coconut aminos, or soy sauce
3 tablespoons (60 g) pure maple syrup
3 tablespoons (45 ml) unseasoned rice vinegar
2 tablespoons (16 g) cornstarch
¼ cup (60 ml) water
4 cups (660 g) cooked rice
Sliced scallions
Sprinkle of sesame seeds

**Yield: 4 servings**

# Roasted Winter Vegetable Bowls with Couscous, Romesco Sauce, and Tahini Drizzle

This recipe may seem like it has a lot of steps, but they are all easy and can basically be done at the same time. While the vegetables are roasting, you can make all other components of the dish so that everything is ready to go when the vegetables are done. The romesco sauce can be made ahead of time and kept in the fridge.

**For the Roasted Vegetables:** Preheat the oven to 400°F (200°C, or gas mark 6). Line a rimmed baking sheet with parchment paper and set aside.

Place all the ingredients in a large mixing bowl and toss well. Spread out onto the prepared baking sheet in one even layer. Roast for 15 minutes, stir the vegetables, and spread back out in one even layer and then roast for 10 to 15 minutes more.

**For the Couscous:** Bring the water to a boil, turn off the heat, and add the olive oil and salt. Pour in the couscous and let it sit for 5 to 10 minutes. When all the water is absorbed, fluff with a fork. Stirring with a spoon may create clumps; a fork is best here.

**For the Spicy Toasted Pumpkin Seeds:** Line a small plate with parchment paper and set aside. Heat the olive oil, maple syrup, cayenne, and garlic powder in a small skillet over medium heat, stirring gently. When you start to see it sizzling, add the pumpkin seeds. Stir frequently until the seeds are toasted, about 4 to 5 minutes. Transfer the pumpkin seeds to the prepared plate. They will continue to crisp up as they sit.

**For the Tahini Drizzle:** Add the tahini, maple syrup, and balsamic vinegar to a small bowl. Stir to combine. Add water 1 tablespoon (15 ml) at a time until the desired consistency is reached.

**To assemble the bowls:** Place 1 cup (30 g) of baby spinach in a bowl, top with one-quarter of the couscous, one-quarter of the roasted vegetables, a generous dollop of Romesco Sauce, 2 tablespoons (18 g) of Spicy Toasted Pumpkin Seeds, and a tablespoon or two of Tahini Drizzle.

> **Tip:** Make this dish gluten-free by using 1 cup (173 g) of quinoa, cooked according to package directions, in place of the couscous.

**FOR ROASTED VEGETABLES:**
2 sweet potatoes, peeled and chopped into 1-inch (2.5 cm) cubes
2 parsnips, peeled and chopped into 1-inch (2.5 cm) cubes
8 radishes, halved or quartered if large
1 red onion, halved and sliced
1 tablespoon (15 ml) olive oil
1 teaspoon dried thyme
¼ teaspoon salt, or to taste
⅛ teaspoon black pepper, or to taste

**FOR COUSCOUS:**
1½ cups (355 ml) water
1 teaspoon olive oil
¼ teaspoon salt, or to taste
1 cup (175 g) dry couscous

**FOR SPICY TOASTED PUMPKIN SEEDS:**
1 teaspoon olive oil
1 teaspoon pure maple syrup
¼ teaspoon cayenne
¼ teaspoon garlic powder
½ cup (70 g) raw shelled pumpkin seeds

**FOR TAHINI DRIZZLE:**
⅓ cup (80 g) tahini
1 tablespoon (20 g) pure maple syrup
1 tablespoon (15 ml) balsamic vinegar
2-4 tablespoons (28-60 ml) water, to thin

**FOR BOWLS:**
4 cups (120 g) baby spinach
1 recipe Romesco Sauce (page 167)
1 recipe Tahini Drizzle

**Yield: 4 servings**

# Green Goddess Quinoa Bowls with Crispy Tofu

Filled with a mix of cooked and raw vegetables, plus nutty red quinoa and tofu, these wholesome bowls are light, yet filling. True to its name, it's finished off with a velvety smooth green goddess dressing. Get a head start by blending together the dressing, cooking the quinoa and tofu, and steaming the broccoli a day in advance, and then reheat just before serving.

1 cup (175 g) red quinoa, rinsed

2 cups (470 ml) water

Kosher salt and freshly ground black pepper

1 tablespoon (14 g) coconut oil

14 ounces (392 g) extra-firm tofu, pressed, drained, and cubed

1 medium head broccoli, cut into florets

1 recipe Avocado Green Goddess Dressing (page 169)

12 thick asparagus spears, ends trimmed and shaved into ribbons

6 ounces (168 g) snap peas, halved

Bean sprouts

Hemp seeds

**Yield: 4 servings**

Combine the quinoa, water, and a generous pinch of salt in a medium saucepan. Bring to a boil, then cover, reduce the heat to low, and simmer until tender, about 15 minutes. Remove from the heat, and steam with the lid on for about 5 minutes.

Heat the oil in a large skillet over medium-high heat until shimmering. Add the tofu, season with salt and pepper, and cook until the bottom is lightly browned and crisp, about 2 minutes. Flip and continue cooking until all sides are browned.

Meanwhile, steam the broccoli.

To serve, stir a spoonful of the dressing into the quinoa, then divide among bowls. Top with tofu, broccoli, asparagus, snap peas, and bean sprouts. Drizzle with Avocado Green Goddess Dressing and sprinkle with hemp seeds.

# Cauliflower Falafel Power Bowls

This nourishing bowl has all the best parts of eating falafel—a generous helping of fresh vegetables, creamy avocado, a scoop of hummus, and something tangy, which in this case is red cabbage sauerkraut. Get a head start by making the falafel up to a couple of days in advance and storing the cooked patties in the fridge, or in the freezer for up to a few months.

3 cups or 2 cans (15 ounce, or 420 g) chickpeas, drained and rinsed
1 small red onion, roughly chopped
2 cloves garlic
2 tablespoons (30 ml) freshly squeezed lemon juice
½ packed cup (24 g) fresh parsley leaves
½ packed cup (8 g) fresh cilantro leaves
2 teaspoons ground cumin
1 teaspoon ground coriander
⅛ teaspoon cayenne pepper
Kosher salt and freshly ground black pepper
3 tablespoons (24 g) all-purpose flour
1 teaspoon baking powder
1 tablespoon (15 ml) avocado or extra-virgin olive oil
16 ounces (455 g) riced cauliflower
2 teaspoons za'atar
2 packed cups (40 g) arugula
1 medium red bell pepper, cored and chopped
2 avocados, peeled, pitted, and diced
Red cabbage or beet sauerkraut
Hummus

**Yield: 4 servings**

If using dried beans, add the chickpeas to a medium bowl and cover with water by at least 1 inch (2.5 cm). Let them sit, uncovered, at room temperature for 24 hours.

Preheat the oven to 375°F (190°C, or gas mark 5).

Add the drained chickpeas, onion, garlic, lemon juice, parsley, cilantro, cumin, coriander, cayenne, 1 teaspoon of salt, and ¼ teaspoon pepper to the bowl of a food processor. Pulse about 10 times until the chickpeas are chopped. Scrape down the sides of the bowl, add the flour and baking powder, and pulse until the mixture is well combined.

Scoop out about 2 tablespoons of the mixture and roll it into a ball in the palms of your hands. Transfer to a lightly greased baking sheet and use a spatula to flatten into a ½-inch (1.3 cm)-thick disc. Repeat with the remainder of the mixture.

Bake the falafel until cooked through and tender, 25 to 30 minutes, flipping once halfway through.

Heat the oil in a large skillet over medium heat. Add the riced cauliflower, za'atar, salt, and pepper, and stir to combine. Cook, stirring occasionally, until the cauliflower is slightly softened, about 3 minutes.

To serve, divide the cauliflower rice and arugula among bowls. Top with falafel patties, bell pepper, avocado, sauerkraut, and a scoop of hummus.

# Herbed Chickpea and Bulgur Bowls

Get a head start on prepping the chickpeas in this recipe and you will be handsomely rewarded. They're tossed with a simple mix of oil, red onion, fresh herbs, and tangy sumac, then left to marinate for as much time as you can spare. (But the result is still quite delicious when prepared shortly before eating.)

Add the chickpeas, oil, onion, herbs, sumac, salt, and pepper to a medium bowl, and stir to combine. Set aside to marinate while you prepare the remainder of the bowl.

Combine the bulgur, water, and a generous pinch of salt in a medium saucepan. Bring to a boil, then cover, reduce the heat to low, and simmer until tender, 10 to 15 minutes. Remove from the heat and stir in the arugula and vinegar.

Meanwhile, steam the broccoli.

To serve, divide the bulgur and cabbage among bowls. Top with chickpeas, broccoli, avocado, and Roasted Red Pepper Sauce.

1½ cups (300 g) or 1 can (15 ounces, or 420 g) chickpeas, drained and rinsed
1 tablespoon (15 ml) avocado or extra-virgin olive oil
¼ cup (40 g) diced red onion
2 tablespoons (6 g) finely chopped parsley
1 tablespoon (1 g) finely chopped cilantro
½ teaspoon sumac
Kosher salt and freshly ground black pepper
¾ cup (125 g) bulgur
1½ cups (355 ml) water
2 packed cups (40 g) arugula
2 teaspoons apple cider vinegar
½ head broccoli, cut into small florets
2 cups (140 g) finely shredded red cabbage
2 avocados, peeled, pitted, and thinly sliced
¾ cup (180 ml) Roasted Red Pepper Sauce (page 173)

**Yield: 4 servings**

# Thai Coconut Curry Bowls

There are some recipes that will win you over with a medley of big, bold, savory flavors, and some that will do it purely on looks alone. This Thai-inspired veggie bowl does both. It's worth noting that most, though not all, brands of red Thai curry paste contain shellfish. Look for brands, like Thai Kitchen, that are shellfish free.

Heat the oil in a medium saucepan over medium heat. Add the garlic and ginger, stir to coat, and cook until fragrant, about 30 seconds. Stir in the curry paste and cook for 1 minute longer. Stir in the coconut milk, stock, and lime zest, and season with salt and pepper. Bring to a boil, then reduce the heat to low and simmer for 15 minutes. Stir in the tofu and green beans, and simmer for 5 minutes longer. Remove from the heat, stir in the tamari, and season to taste.

Meanwhile, steam the broccoli.

To serve, divide the zucchini noodles among bowls. Top with tofu and green beans, broccoli, and cabbage. Pour the curry sauce over the top, sprinkle with peanuts and cilantro, and add a squeeze of lime juice.

1 tablespoon (14 g) coconut oil

3 cloves garlic, minced

1½ tablespoons (9 g) finely chopped fresh ginger

2 tablespoons (30 g) red Thai curry paste

1 can (14 ounces, or 392 g) unsweetened coconut milk

1½ cups (355 ml) vegetable stock

1 lime, zested, then cut into wedges

Kosher salt and freshly ground black pepper

14 ounces (392 g) extra-firm tofu, pressed, drained, and cubed

8 ounces (225 g) green beans, trimmed

2 teaspoons tamari

1 head broccoli, cut into florets

16 ounces (455 g) zucchini noodles

1 cup (70 g) shredded red cabbage

Roasted unsalted peanuts, chopped

Chopped fresh cilantro

**Yield: 4 servings**

# Chili-Maple Tofu Bowls

This Buddha bowl has lots of eye-catching colors, a mélange of different textures, and a mix of balanced, bright flavors that will awaken your taste buds. The level of heat is really up to you, as much of it comes from the Spicy Peanut Sauce (swapping the sriracha for garlic chili sauce or sambal oelek). All of the ingredients can be prepped and cooked in advance, but wait until right before serving to add the sauce.

1 cup (235 ml) rice vinegar

1 cup (235 ml) water

¼ teaspoon red pepper flakes

Kosher salt and freshly ground black pepper

3 medium carrots, peeled and shaved into ribbons

¼ cup (60 ml) tamari

2 tablespoons (30 ml) maple syrup

2 teaspoons garlic chili sauce

14 ounces (392 g) extra-firm tofu, pressed, drained, and cut into triangles

8 ounces (225 g) buckwheat soba noodles

1 tablespoon (15 ml) avocado or extra-virgin olive oil

1 cup (70 g) finely shredded red cabbage

1 cup (120 g) shelled edamame

2 avocados, peeled, pitted, and thinly sliced

¾ cup (180 ml) Spicy Peanut Sauce (page 172)

3 scallions, green parts only, thinly sliced

**Yield: 4 servings**

Bring the vinegar, water, red pepper flakes, and 1 teaspoon salt to a boil in a medium saucepan, stirring to dissolve the salt. Pour the hot liquid over the carrots in a medium bowl; set aside.

Whisk together the tamari, maple syrup, and garlic chili sauce in a shallow container. Add the tofu and stir to coat. Marinate for at least 10 minutes.

Bring a large pot of salted water to a boil. Add the soba noodles and cook according to the package instructions. Drain and rinse well with cool water.

Drain the marinade from the tofu. Heat the oil in a large skillet over medium-high heat until shimmering. Add the tofu, season with salt and pepper, and cook until the bottom is lightly browned and crisp, about 2 minutes. Flip and continue cooking until all sides are lightly browned.

To serve, drain the liquid from the carrots. Divide the soba noodles among bowls. Top with tofu wedges, pickled carrot ribbons, red cabbage, edamame, and avocado. Drizzle with Spicy Peanut Sauce and sprinkle with scallions.

# Moroccan-Spiced Chickpea Bowls

These saucy, spiced chickpea bowls are all the proof you need that comfort food can also be healthy. Humble chickpeas are the star of the bowl, accented with harissa and a medley of cumin, paprika, and cinnamon. Harissa is a North African chili paste that's both smoky and spicy. A little can go a long way, so if you prefer something a little more mild, use about half the amount of harissa called for.

Heat 2 tablespoons (30 ml) of the oil in a skillet over medium heat until shimmering. Add the onion and cook, stirring occasionally, until soft and fragrant, about 5 minutes. Stir in the garlic, harissa, tomato paste, cumin, paprika, cinnamon, salt, and pepper, and cook for 2 minutes. Stir in the chickpeas and tomatoes. Bring to a boil, then reduce the heat to low and simmer for 20 minutes. Meanwhile, prepare the bulgur.

Combine the bulgur, water, and a generous pinch of salt in a medium saucepan. Bring to a boil. Reduce the heat to low, cover, and simmer until tender, 10 to 15 minutes.

Heat the remaining 1 tablespoon (15 ml) of oil in a skillet over medium heat until shimmering. Add the kale and season with salt. Cook, stirring occasionally, until soft and wilted, about 5 minutes.

To serve, divide the bulgur among bowls. Top with chickpeas and tomatoes, kale, avocado, and an egg. Drizzle with Mint Yogurt Sauce.

3 tablespoons (45 ml) avocado or extra-virgin olive oil, divided
½ medium onion, diced
2 cloves garlic, minced
2 teaspoons harissa
1 teaspoon tomato paste
2 teaspoons ground cumin
1 teaspoon paprika
½ teaspoon ground cinnamon
Kosher salt and freshly ground black pepper
2 cups (400 g) chickpeas, drained
1 can (14 ounces, or 392 g) diced tomatoes
¾ cup (125 g) bulgur
1½ cups (355 ml) water
8 packed cups (560 g) shredded kale
2 avocados, peeled, pitted, and thinly sliced
4 poached eggs
1 recipe Mint Yogurt Sauce (page 175)

**Yield: 4 servings**

# Winter Squash and Farro Macro Bowls

If you're not already familiar with this winter squash, delicata is small with an elongated shape, a mild-mannered, not-too-sweet flavor, and covered with a thin, yellow-and-green-striped skin that is totally edible. For a fun twist, here the rings of squash are blanketed with a thin slick of red curry paste. It offsets the sweetness of the vegetable with the subtlest touch of heat. Try this pairing once, and you'll make it again and again.

1 cup (165 g) pearled farro
3½ cups (822 ml) water, divided
Kosher salt and freshly ground
   black pepper
½ cup (25 g) dried mung beans, rinsed
2 tablespoons (30 ml) avocado or
   extra-virgin olive oil, divided
½ tablespoon (7 g) vegetarian Thai red
   curry paste
2 medium delicata squash
1 bunch rainbow chard, shredded
½ tablespoon (3 g) grated fresh ginger
2 medium beets, peeled and thinly sliced
Crumbled goat cheese
Toasted pumpkin seeds
1 recipe Cilantro-Parsley Pesto
   (page 156)

**Yield: 4 servings**

Preheat the oven to 400°F (200°C, or gas mark 6).

Add the farro, 2 cups (470 ml) of the water, and a generous pinch of salt to a medium saucepan. Bring to a boil, then reduce the heat to low, cover, and simmer until the farro is tender with a slight chew, about 30 minutes.

Add the mung beans, remaining 1½ cups (355 ml) water, and a generous pinch of salt to a separate saucepan. Bring to a boil. Reduce the heat to medium-low and simmer until tender, about 25 minutes. Meanwhile, prepare the vegetables.

Whisk together 1 tablespoon (15 ml) of the oil, curry paste, salt, and pepper in a large bowl. Slice the squash in half lengthwise. Scoop out the seeds. Slice crosswise into ½-inch (1.3 cm)-thick crescents. Add the squash to the bowl and toss to combine. Arrange in a single layer on a rimmed baking sheet, and roast until tender and browned around the edges, 25 minutes, flipping once halfway through.

Heat the remaining 1 tablespoon (15 ml) oil in a large skillet over medium heat. Add the chard, ginger, and salt. Cook, tossing occasionally, until wilted, about 5 minutes.

To serve, divide the farro among bowls. Top with mung beans, roasted squash, chard, beets, goat cheese, pumpkin seeds, and pesto.

## 7

# PERFECT PASTAS

Pasta is the magical ingredient that brings kids to the table time and time again. It's quick, easy, inexpensive, and incredibly versatile. It can stand alone or be used in soups and salads. It's the secret to turning basic ingredients into a meal. Feel free to use gluten-free options with any of the recipes in this chapter.

# Pasta with Eggplant in Tomato Cream Sauce

Though eggplant doesn't have to be peeled, the skin can be a bit tough sometimes. Once it's peeled, you're left with a sponge that soaks up all the yummy flavors you throw its way. In this dish, it becomes "meaty" and filling.

**FOR CASHEW CREAM:**

1 cup (140 g) raw cashews, soaked in hot water for at least 30 minutes

1 cup (235 ml) water

**FOR PASTA AND EGGPLANT:**

12 ounces (340 g) rigatoni or penne

2 tablespoons (28 ml) olive oil

½ yellow onion, diced

2 cloves garlic, minced

1 globe eggplant, peeled and chopped into 1-inch (2.5 cm) pieces (about 4 cups [328 g] chopped)

1 teaspoon dried oregano

½ teaspoon dried basil

¼ teaspoon crushed red pepper flakes, or more to taste

1 can (28 ounces, or 785 g) crushed tomatoes

½ cup (120 ml) low-sodium vegetable broth

1 teaspoon organic white sugar

1 teaspoon salt, or to taste

½ teaspoon black pepper

1 teaspoon balsamic vinegar

½ cup Cashew Cream (recipe above)

Big handful of baby spinach

**Yield: 4 servings**

**Note:** Cashew Cream is easier to make in a large batch, which is why we are making more than we need. Add the remainder to soups and sauces, drizzle it over casseroles, or add a bit of powdered sugar and drizzle it on oatmeal, pancakes, or granola bars as "icing."

**For the Cashew Cream:** Add the soaked cashews and water to a high-speed blender and blend until smooth. Reserve ½ cup (120 ml) and store the rest in an airtight container in the fridge for 3 to 4 days. You can use it just like you would heavy cream or half-and-half.

**For the Pasta and Eggplant:** Cook the pasta according to package directions.

Meanwhile, heat the olive oil in a large, deep skillet over medium heat. Add the onion and sauté for 4 to 5 minutes until soft and translucent. Add the garlic and sauté for 1 minute.

Add the eggplant, oregano, basil, and crushed red pepper flakes. Cook for 5 minutes until the eggplant is starting to soften. Add the crushed tomatoes, vegetable broth, sugar, salt, and pepper and simmer for 15 to 20 minutes.

Add the balsamic vinegar and ½ cup (120 ml) of Cashew Cream and stir well to combine. Add the spinach and stir until it starts to wilt a bit, about 1 to 2 minutes.

Serve the sauce over the noodles.

# Rigatoni with Romesco and Broccoli

It doesn't get much easier than this. Make the Romesco Sauce while the pasta water comes to a boil. Chop the broccoli into florets during the first few minutes of pasta cooking time. Combine and eat! The smoky Spanish-inspired Romesco Sauce is a nice change of pace from typical marinara flavors.

Cook the pasta according to package directions, making sure to salt the cooking water well. When there is 4 minutes left for the pasta, add the broccoli florets to the pasta water. Drain the pasta and broccoli together when done. Add back to the pot, pour in the Romesco Sauce, and stir to ensure everything is evenly coated.

Season with salt and pepper, if desired.

12 ounces (340 g) rigatoni pasta, or other tube-shaped pasta
2 cups (142 g) broccoli florets
1 recipe Romesco Sauce (page 167)
Salt and black pepper (optional)

**Yield: 4 servings**

# Rotini with Chunky Garden Veggie Marinara

This is a great sauce for when your backyard garden is plentiful with ripe veggies. Feel free to use the vegetables you have available. Use summer squash instead of the zucchini, double up on the carrots and leave out the peppers, or swap the eggplant for meaty mushrooms. Make it your own!

Cook the pasta according to package directions.

Heat the olive oil over medium heat in a large skillet. Add the onion and sauté for 5 to 6 minutes until soft and translucent. Add the garlic and sauté for 1 minute.

Add the zucchini, eggplant, carrot, and bell pepper and sauté for 7 to 8 minutes until the vegetables start to soften. Add a tablespoon or two (15 to 28 ml) of vegetable broth if the skillet gets dry.

Add the crushed tomatoes, salt, pepper, basil, balsamic vinegar, and ¼ cup (60 ml) of vegetable broth. Stir to combine. Simmer the sauce on low heat for 20 minutes, stirring occasionally.

Serve the sauce over the cooked noodles.

12 ounces (340 g) rotini pasta or pasta of choice
2 tablespoons (28 ml) olive oil
1 yellow onion, diced
2 cloves garlic, minced
1 small zucchini, diced
¾ cup peeled and diced eggplant (about ½ globe eggplant)
1 large carrot, peeled and diced
1 red bell pepper, seeded and diced
1 can (28 ounces, or 785 g) crushed tomatoes
1 teaspoon salt, or to taste
¼ teaspoon black pepper, or to taste
2 teaspoons dried basil
1 tablespoon (15 ml) balsamic vinegar
¼ cup (60 ml) low-sodium vegetable broth, plus more if needed

**Yield: 6 servings**

# Lentil Bolognese with Spaghetti

This Bolognese is so easy it will become one of your go-to meals. It contains healthy plant-based protein and fiber, but go ahead and serve with a simple salad and garlic bread to complete the meal.

Cook the spaghetti according to package directions.

Heat the olive oil over medium heat in a large skillet. Add the onion and sauté until soft and translucent, about 5 to 6 minutes. Add the mushrooms and sauté for 7 to 8 minutes until soft and cooked through, stirring occasionally.

Add the wine and sauté until no liquid is left, stirring occasionally. Add the crushed tomatoes, vegetable broth, balsamic vinegar, tamari, parsley, basil, oregano, salt, and pepper. Stir to combine. Reduce the heat to medium-low and simmer for 15 minutes. Add the cooked lentils and stir to combine. Cook for another 2 to 3 minutes to heat through.

Serve warm over the spaghetti.

16 ounces (455 g) spaghetti noodles or pasta of choice
1 tablespoon (15 ml) olive oil
½ sweet onion, diced
10 ounces (280 g) cremini mushrooms, finely diced
¼ cup (60 ml) robust dry red wine (optional)
1 can (28 ounces, or 785 g) crushed tomatoes
½ cup (120 ml) low-sodium vegetable broth
2 tablespoons (28 ml) balsamic vinegar
1 tablespoon (15 ml) tamari, coconut aminos, or soy sauce
2 tablespoons (2 g) dried parsley
1 tablespoon (5 g) dried basil
2 teaspoons dried oregano
1 teaspoon salt, or to taste
¼ teaspoon black pepper, or to taste
1 cup (198 g) cooked brown or green lentils

**Yield: 6 servings**

# Vegan Scampi in Lemon Garlic White Wine Sauce

This is a really simple dish that tastes elegant. Hearts of palm are the perfect stand-in for scallops. They have a similar look when sliced and a briny quality reminiscent of seafood—great for those with a shellfish allergy.

1 jar (14.8 ounces, or 420 g) hearts of palm

3 tablespoons (45 ml) olive oil, divided

½ teaspoon salt, divided

¼ teaspoon black pepper, divided

8 ounces (225 g) linguine or pasta of choice

4 cloves garlic, minced

½ cup (120 ml) dry white wine (see Note)

Juice of 1 lemon

1 cup (235 ml) low-sodium vegetable broth

Handful of fresh parsley, chopped

Pinch of crushed red pepper flakes (optional)

2 tablespoons (6 g) panko bread crumbs

1 tablespoon (4 g) nutritional yeast (optional)

**Yield: 4 servings**

**Note:** If you're avoiding alcohol, use the same amount of vegetable broth with 2 tablespoons (28 ml) of white wine vinegar.

Fill a large pasta pot with water and bring to a boil.

Meanwhile, carefully slice the hearts of palm crosswise into ½-inch (1 cm) slices.

Heat 1 tablespoon (15 ml) of olive oil in a large skillet over medium-high heat. Once the oil is hot, add the hearts of palm. Sprinkle with ¼ teaspoon of salt and ⅛ teaspoon of pepper. Sear until golden brown, about 2 to 3 minutes. Gently flip each slice over. Sprinkle with the remaining ¼ teaspoon of salt and ⅛ teaspoon of pepper. Sear for another 2 to 3 minutes until golden brown. Transfer to a plate.

Drop the pasta in the boiling water and cook according to package directions.

Meanwhile, heat the remaining 2 tablespoons (28 ml) of olive oil over medium heat. Sauté the garlic for 1 to 2 minutes. Add the white wine and simmer for 3 to 4 minutes until the liquid reduces by about half. Add the lemon juice and vegetable broth and simmer for 5 minutes until reduced and glossy.

Add the cooked pasta to the skillet and toss to combine. Add the seared hearts of palm to the skillet along with the parsley and crushed red pepper flakes, if using.

Stir together the panko bread crumbs and the nutritional yeast, if using. Sprinkle over the pasta and toss everything to combine.

# Butternut Squash Mac and Cheese

Macaroni noodles are drenched in a creamy, cheesy pasta sauce with hidden veggies that no one will detect. It's a family favorite. It even survived a kids' taste test on national TV. Spoiler alert: They all loved it!

Make the Butternut Mac Cheese Sauce according to directions.

Cook the macaroni noodles according to package directions. Drain, then add the pasta back to the pot.

Add the Butternut Mac Cheese Sauce to the pasta and stir well to combine.

**1 recipe Butternut Mac Cheese Sauce (page 168)**
**12 ounces (340 g) macaroni noodles**

**Yield: 4 to 6 servings**

**Note:** Frozen peas are a great addition. Simply add them to the strainer and drain the pasta over them. Fresh spinach would also work great.

# COMFORTING CASSEROLES

Casseroles are like a big hug. They're warm, inviting, and comforting. Once everything is in the baking dish, all you must do is wait patiently for it to get hot and bubbly in the oven. Use this time to help the kids with their homework, respond to emails, or pop open a bottle of wine!

# Potpie Noodle Casserole

This is just like potpie, but without the fuss of a pie crust. Bonus: there are noodles in this casserole that you don't get in traditional potpie. Your family will go crazy for this dish.

**FOR POTPIE NOODLES:**

8 ounces (225 g) rotini or other medium shape pasta, such as rigatoni

2 tablespoons (28 ml) olive oil

1 yellow onion, diced

2 ribs celery, diced

2 tablespoons (16 g) all-purpose flour (see Note)

1 tablespoon (6 g) Italian seasoning

3 tablespoons (45 ml) tamari, coconut aminos, or soy sauce

¼ teaspoon salt, or to taste

¼ teaspoon black pepper, or to taste

2 cups (475 ml) low-sodium vegetable broth

1 package (16 ounces, or 455 g) frozen mixed vegetables (corn, peas, carrots, and green beans)

1 cup (235 ml) cashew milk or other creamy nondairy milk (such as lite coconut or unsweetened soy)

2 tablespoons (8 g) nutritional yeast (optional)

**FOR GARLIC BREAD CRUMBS:**

¼ cup (13 g) panko bread crumbs or regular bread crumbs

¼ cup (15 g) nutritional yeast or more bread crumbs

1 teaspoon granulated garlic powder

1 tablespoon (15 g) melted butter or coconut oil

**Yield: 4 to 6 servings**

**Note:** Use brown rice flour or a gluten-free flour blend instead of all-purpose flour for a gluten-free option. Feel free to add a 15-ounce (425 g) can of drained and rinsed chickpeas for added protein.

Preheat the oven to 350°F (180°C, or gas mark 4).

**For the Potpie Noodles:** Cook the rotini to al dente, according to package directions. Drain and set aside.

Meanwhile, heat the olive oil over medium heat in a large, deep skillet. Add the onion and celery. Sauté for 5 to 6 minutes until softened and the onion is translucent. Add the flour and stir until combined and no flour is visible. Add the Italian seasoning, tamari, salt, and pepper and stir to combine.

Slowly pour in the vegetable broth, whisking continuously to ensure a smooth sauce. Add the mixed vegetables, cashew milk, and nutritional yeast, if using. Stir to combine, bring to a simmer, and cook for a few minutes to thicken. Add the cooked rotini and stir again to combine. Transfer the mixture to a 9- × 13-inch (23 × 33 cm) baking dish.

**For the Garlic Bread Crumbs:** In a small bowl, stir together the panko bread crumbs, nutritional yeast, and garlic powder. Pour the melted butter over the bread crumb mixture while stirring to moisten thoroughly.

Sprinkle the Garlic Bread Crumbs over the top of the casserole. Bake for 20 to 25 minutes until the bread crumbs are toasted and the sauce is thick and bubbly.

# Vegetarian Lentil Cottage Pie

This is not your typical shepherd's pie. Made with lentils, butternut squash, cauliflower, and spices in a rich savory tomato sauce and topped off with creamy carrot mashed potatoes, this is comfort food at its best!

**FOR FILLING:**

1½ cups (210 g) peeled and diced butternut squash

1½ cups (150 g) cauliflower florets

2 tablespoons (28 ml) olive oil

1 onion, diced

2 cloves garlic, minced

3 tablespoons (48 g) tomato paste

2 tablespoons (28 ml) vegan Worcestershire sauce

2 tablespoons (28 ml) tamari, coconut aminos, or soy sauce

1½ teaspoons dried thyme

1 teaspoon salt, or to taste

¼ teaspoon black pepper, or to taste

1½ cups (355 ml) low-sodium vegetable broth, plus more as needed

2 cups (396 g) cooked brown or green lentils

**FOR MASH:**

4 cups (440 g) diced and peeled potatoes (preferably Yukon Gold)

2 carrots, peeled and diced

2 cloves garlic, minced

1 tablespoon (15 ml) olive oil

1 teaspoon salt, or to taste

Unsweetened milk of choice to thin, if needed

**Yield: 6 servings**

Preheat the oven to 400°F (200°C, or gas mark 6). Lightly spray a 2½-quart (2.4 L) casserole dish with cooking spray and set aside.

Place the butternut squash and cauliflower in a pot and add enough water to cover the vegetables. Cover, bring to a boil, reduce the heat, and simmer for about 15 to 20 minutes until tender, but not mushy. Drain.

**For the Mash:** Meanwhile, place the potatoes and carrots in a pot with enough water to cover them. Cover, bring to a boil, and then reduce the heat and simmer for 15 to 20 minutes until the vegetables are very soft. Drain and return to the pot. Add the garlic, olive oil, and salt. Using a potato masher, mash the vegetables until smooth; the carrots may not get as smooth as the potatoes and that's okay, just mash them as best you can. Add a splash or two of milk to thin, if needed.

**For the Filling:** In a large skillet on the stove, heat 2 tablespoons (28 ml) olive oil over medium heat. Add the onion and sauté until translucent, about 5 to 6 minutes. Add the garlic and sauté for 1 minute. Add the tomato paste, Worcestershire sauce, tamari, thyme, salt, and pepper. Stir to combine and cook for another 2 to 3 minutes.

Add the vegetable broth, lentils, and squash-cauliflower mixture and stir to combine. Simmer for 5 to 10 minutes until the mixture is thick but saucy. If this mixture seems too thick, add another ¼ to ½ cup (60 to 120 ml) of vegetable broth to loosen it up.

Pour the lentil filling in the casserole dish and spread evenly. Spoon the mashed potato mixture over the top and spread until even. Be careful not to press down too hard or the potatoes will end up in the filling instead of on top of it. Alternatively, you could let the filling cool first before adding the potatoes to the top. Bake for 20 minutes until hot and bubbly.

# Black Bean and Zucchini Enchiladas

These enchiladas are always a hit! They are so easy to make, but they taste like total comfort food. The sauce is an easy, nontraditional blend of white beans and salsa, bringing even more plant-based protein to the party. You will not miss the cheese!

Preheat the oven to 350°F (180°C, or gas mark 4).

Heat the olive oil in a skillet over medium heat. Sauté the onion until translucent, about 5 to 6 minutes. Add the garlic, bell pepper, zucchini, 1 teaspoon of cumin, and ¼ teaspoon of salt and sauté for 2 minutes. Add the black beans and stir to combine. Turn the heat to low to keep warm while you make the sauce.

Combine the salsa, white beans, 1 teaspoon of cumin, chili powder, water, and ¼ teaspoon of salt in a blender or food processor. Purée until smooth.

Add 1 cup (235 ml) of the sauce to the black bean–zucchini mixture and stir to combine.

Pour ½ cup (120 ml) of the sauce in the bottom of a 7- × 11-inch (18 × 28 cm) baking dish.

Place about ⅓ cup (90 g) of filling in one tortilla, roll up, and place seam-side down in the baking dish. Repeat with the remaining tortillas.

Top the enchiladas with the remaining sauce and any remaining filling. Bake for 20 minutes. Garnish with your toppings of choice.

**Tip:** Add 1 cup (164 g) of corn kernels to the filling, if desired. Slightly warming the tortillas will make them more pliable for folding.

1 tablespoon (15 ml) olive oil
½ red onion, diced
2 cloves garlic, minced
1 red bell pepper, seeded and diced
½ zucchini, diced (about 1 cup [120 g])
2 teaspoons ground cumin, divided
½ teaspoon salt, divided, or to taste
1 can (15 ounces, or 425 g) black beans, rinsed and drained (or 1½ cups [258 g] cooked beans)
1 jar (16 ounces, or 455 g) tomato-based salsa
1 can (15 ounces, or 425 g) cannellini beans (white kidney beans), rinsed and drained (or 1½ cups [267 g] cooked beans)
½ teaspoon chili powder
½ cup (120 ml) water or low-sodium vegetable broth
8 corn or flour tortillas (corn tortillas for gluten-free)

TOPPINGS OF CHOICE (OPTIONAL):
BEST Guacamole (page 165)
Creamy Cumin Ranch Dressing (page 164)
Sliced jalapeños
Cilantro
Diced tomatoes

**Yield: 4 servings**

# Tortilla Enchilada Casserole

The combination of the savory, smoky enchilada sauce and subtly sweet dressing is a winner. This casserole is loaded with healthy veggies and filling beans. And kids will love it, too!

Preheat the oven to 350°F (180°C, or gas mark 4).

**For the Enchilada Sauce:** Combine all the ingredients in a small pot over medium-high heat. When it starts to bubble, reduce the heat to low and simmer for 10 to 15 minutes. Set aside.

**For the Casserole:** Meanwhile, heat the olive oil in a large skillet over medium heat. Add the onion and sauté for 5 to 6 minutes until softened and translucent. Add the garlic, zucchini, bell peppers, corn, cumin, oregano, salt, and pepper and sauté for 5 to 6 minutes until softened.

Pour ¼ cup (60 ml) of the Enchilada Sauce in the bottom of an 8- × 8-inch (20 × 20 cm) baking dish. Lay 4 pieces of tortilla on the sauce, flat side against the sides of the baking dish. Use 6 pieces if you're using corn tortillas; get creative and fill the spaces to cover the bottom of the dish. The curved sides will overlap each other a bit. Spread half of the vegetable mixture on top, followed by half of the black beans.

Repeat the process, laying the other 4 pieces of tortillas on top of the beans like before, followed by ¼ cup (60 ml) of Enchilada Sauce, the remaining vegetables, and the remaining beans. Dollop ½ cup (120 ml) of the Creamy Cumin Ranch Dressing over the top and carefully spread it out with a spatula.

Place the baking dish on a cookie sheet to prevent spills and bake for 20 minutes until hot.

**FOR ENCHILADA SAUCE:**

1 can (15 ounces, or 425 g) tomato sauce
½ cup (120 ml) low-sodium vegetable broth
2 tablespoons (16 g) chili powder
1 teaspoon ground cumin
1½ teaspoons smoked paprika
½ teaspoon salt, or to taste
½ teaspoon onion powder
¼ teaspoon dried oregano
Pinch of cayenne (optional), for extra heat

**FOR CASSEROLE:**

2 tablespoons (28 ml) olive oil
1 yellow onion, diced
2 cloves garlic, minced
1 zucchini, diced
1 red bell pepper, seeded and diced
1 orange or yellow pepper, seeded and diced (or another red bell pepper)
1 cup (164 g) fresh or frozen corn kernels
1 teaspoon ground cumin
½ teaspoon dried oregano
½ teaspoon salt, or to taste
¼ teaspoon black pepper, or to taste
4 flour tortillas (8 inches, or 20 cm each) or 6 corn tortillas (6 inches, or 15 cm each) for gluten-free, cut in half
1 can (15 ounces, or 425 g) black beans, rinsed and drained
1 recipe Creamy Cumin Ranch Dressing (page 164)

**Yield: 6 servings**

# Pesto Lasagna

Your family won't get enough of this lasagna! The pesto is so flavorful and magically imparts a "cheesy" flavor. Omnivores and carnivores alike will love this recipe.

1 package (14 ounces, or 390 g) firm or extra-firm tofu, drained

1 recipe Quick and Easy Marinara Sauce (page 166)

1 recipe Mixed Greens Pepita Pesto (page 157)

1 tablespoon (15 ml) apple cider vinegar

½ teaspoon salt, or to taste

9–10 oven-ready lasagna noodles

½ cup (25 g) panko bread crumbs

½ teaspoon garlic powder

½ teaspoon dried oregano

1 tablespoon (15 ml) melted butter or coconut oil

**Yield: 6 servings**

Preheat the oven to 350°F (180°C, or gas mark 4).

Press the tofu for 20 minutes. Wrap the block of tofu in several paper towels or a clean kitchen towel and place on a plate. Place another plate on top of the tofu and weigh down the top plate. A heavy skillet or cans or bags of beans or rice work well for this. This tower may start to topple as the tofu loses liquid, so don't use anything breakable, like glass jars, as a weight.

Meanwhile, make the Quick and Easy Marinara Sauce and set aside.

While the sauce is simmering, make the Mixed Greens Pepita Pesto, adding the apple cider vinegar and salt.

In a food processor, combine the pressed tofu and the prepared pesto. Process until combined well.

In an 8- × 11-inch (20 × 28 cm) casserole dish, ladle 1 cup (235 ml) of Quick and Easy Marinara Sauce in the bottom. On top, place 3 lasagna noodles, trying not to overlap, although a slight overlap is fine. Break off pieces of a fourth noodle to fill in any remaining spaces on the sides. Dollop 1½ cups (390 g) of the pesto mixture on top of the first layer of noodles and gently spread it out to cover all the noodles. Pour 1 cup (235 ml) of the Quick and Easy Marinara Sauce on top of the pesto and gently spread it out evenly. Repeat with 3 more noodles, the rest of the pesto mixture, and another 1 cup (235 ml) of Quick and Easy Marinara Sauce. Finish with the final 3 noodles, again breaking up an extra one to fill in any spaces, if necessary, and follow with 1 more cup (235 ml) of the Quick and Easy Marinara Sauce.

Cover the casserole dish with aluminum foil and bake for 30 minutes.

Meanwhile, in a small bowl, combine the panko bread crumbs, garlic powder, and oregano. Mix well. Pour the melted butter over the bread crumbs while stirring to thoroughly moisten all of them.

After 30 minutes of baking, uncover the lasagna and evenly sprinkle on the bread crumbs. Bake for another 8 to 10 minutes until the bread crumbs are toasted and golden brown.

Cut into squares and serve with the remaining Quick and Easy Marinara Sauce.

*9*

# AWESOME SIDES

While this book celebrates the awesomeness that is vegetables as main dish, still, we are creatures of habit. We often NEED that extra side of something—something with a different texture, maybe a bit salty or with a different flavor profile, or even something that's just different from what our main course is. Veggies adore these sides, and you will too.

# Smoky Potato Wedges

These smoky potato wedges are addicting!

**To make the seasoning:** Add all the ingredients to a spice grinder (or a clean coffee grinder, or very dry blender) and grind into a fine powder. Set aside.

Preheat the oven to 425°F (220°C, or gas mark 7). Have ready a baking sheet lined with parchment.

**To make the potato wedges:** Cut each potato into 8 to 12 wedges, depending on desired thickness. Rinse the potatoes under cool water and pat dry.

Add the oil, vinegar, and liquid smoke to a large bowl. Add the wedges and toss to coat. Add the seasoning to the bowl and toss to evenly coat.

Arrange the wedges in a single layer and bake for 45 to 50 minutes, flipping halfway through. Serve hot.

**FOR SWEET & SMOKY SEASONING:**

2 tablespoons (16 g) potato starch

1 tablespoon (14 g) tightly packed brown sugar

½ teaspoon smoked salt

¼ teaspoon garlic powder

¼ teaspoon onion powder

¼ teaspoon smoked paprika

¼ teaspoon black pepper

**FOR POTATO WEDGES:**

4 large russet potatoes

2 tablespoons (28 ml) mild-flavored vegetable oil

2 tablespoons (30 ml) apple cider vinegar

1 teaspoon liquid smoke

**Yield: 4 servings**

# Baked Sweet Potato Fries

These fries would go fantastically with pretty much any recipe in this book.

Preheat the oven to 350°F (180°C, or gas mark 4). Line a baking sheet with foil. Line a plate with paper towels. Wash and pat dry the potatoes. Cut the potatoes into fry shapes: wedges, steak fries, skinny fries … it's totally a personal preference. Arrange the fries on the prepared baking sheet. Sprinkle with salt and pepper to taste, and liberally drizzle with olive oil.

Bake for 20 minutes, then rotate them on the baking sheet and bake for 20 minutes longer.

Transfer to the plate to absorb excess oil.

1 large or 2 small yams or sweet potatoes, peeled if desired

Salt and pepper

Olive oil, for drizzling

**Yield: 2 to 4 servings**

# Fried Zucchini

Now's your chance to try out the slicing attachment on your food processor. Dang if it won't slice your zucchini into a bajillion little discs in a matter of 6 seconds.

2 or 3 zucchini, sliced into rounds
1 cup (125 g) all-purpose flour
½ teaspoon paprika
½ teaspoon cayenne pepper
½ teaspoon dried parsley
Salt and pepper
Oil, for frying

**Yield: 4 servings**

Place the zukes, flour, paprika, cayenne, parsley, and salt and pepper to taste in a large zipper-seal bag and shake until you get a nice coating on each piece. Line a plate with paper towels.

Preheat ¼ inch (6 mm) oil in a cast-iron skillet over high heat. The oil is ready when a piece of dough dropped into it sizzles immediately. Fry these puppies until golden, 1 to 2 minutes per side. Make sure you don't overcrowd the pan.

Remove from the oil with a slotted spoon and transfer to the plate to absorb excess oil.

Pop 'em back into the bag for a fresh coating of the flour mixture.

Meanwhile, add a little bit more oil to the pan and let it heat back up. Then, for the second fry. This time, cook a little longer on each side, to get that yummy golden brown color. After the second fry, it's back to the draining plate.

Serve with Quick and Easy Marinara Sauce (page 166), chunky style if desired, for dipping.

# Totchos

Nachos are great, but Totchos, topped with baked potato toppings, are what you want with a burger. This recipe is family size. Make it in a casserole for the whole gang to munch on. And if you think tater tots are passé, swap 'em out for Smoky Potato Wedges (page 143).

2 pounds (908 g) frozen tater tots
1 recipe Cheezy Sauce (page 67)
1 cup (100 g) imitation bacon bits,
    store-bought or homemade
    (page 176)
½ cup (120 g) sour cream, store-bought
    or homemade nondairy (page 162)
½ cup (50 g) chopped green onions

**Yield: 8 servings**

Preheat the oven to 450°F (230°C, or gas mark 8). Have ready a 3 x 9 x 2-inch (7.5 x 23 x 5 cm) baking dish or casserole dish.

Arrange the tots in a single layer and bake 28 to 32 minutes, tossing halfway through, or until golden brown and crisp. Carefully remove from the oven. (You can also opt to cook these in a deep fryer for an even more restaurant-style tot.)

Ladle the Cheezy Sauce all over the top. Sprinkle evenly with bacon bits. Drop dollops of sour cream all over. Sprinkle on the green onions. Serve immediately.

# Dill Pickle Potato Smashers

Have you heard? Dill pickle–flavored everything is all the rage these days. Everything from popsicles to candy canes! Dill pickle potato chips are the inspiration for these potato smashers, except they're not fried and crispy … rather baked and creamy with that salty vinegar punch.

Preheat the oven to 450°F (230°C, or gas mark 8). Line a baking sheet with parchment or a silicone baking mat.

Add the potatoes and coarse salt to a medium pot. Cover with water and bring to a boil. Reduce the heat and simmer until the potatoes are fork-tender, about 20 minutes.

Drain and return the potatoes to the pot. Add the butter and gently toss to coat.

Arrange the potatoes in a single layer on the baking sheet. Smash each potato into a disc about ½ inch (1.3 cm) thick using a potato masher or the bottom of a heavy-bottomed drinking glass.

Bake for 20 minutes. Remove from the oven and flip. Drizzle with olive oil and bake for an additional 20 minutes.

Remove from the oven and immediately sprinkle with vinegar, chopped chives, dill, and salt and pepper. Serve hot.

2 pounds (908 g) baby red potatoes, with skin on
1 tablespoon (18 g) coarse sea salt
2 tablespoons (28 g) butter
2 tablespoons (28 ml) olive oil
2 tablespoons (30 ml) white vinegar
2 tablespoons (13 g) chopped fresh chives (optional)
2 teaspoons dried dill, or 2 tablespoons (7 g) fresh chopped dill
Additional salt and pepper, to taste

**Yield: 4 servings**

# Green Bean Fries

Green beans are good, but FRIED green beans are better!

Heat oil to 350°F (180°C). Have ready a plate lined with paper towels.

In a medium bowl, mix together the flour, sesame seeds, baking powder, and baking soda.

Add the club soda and sesame oil. Mix until just combined and still lumpy. Take care not to overmix.

Coat the green beans in the batter and fry, a few at a time, until the batter is golden and crispy, about 1 minute. Transfer to the paper towel–lined plate to absorb excess oil. Serve immediately.

Oil, for frying
1¼ cups (156 g) all-purpose flour
1 tablespoon (8 g) black sesame seeds
¼ teaspoon baking powder
¼ teaspoon baking soda
1 cup (235 ml) club soda
1 tablespoon (15 ml) toasted sesame oil
½ pound (227 g) fresh green beans, ends trimmed

**Yield: 2 to 4 servings**

# Buffalo Cauli-Tots

Don't worry, there's still some potato in these tots. But half of the potatoes have been replaced with riced cauliflower to give these little nuggets of crunchy goodness some extra nutrition, you know, since we are going to be dousing them in buttery buffalo sauce.

**2 medium russet potatoes**
**1½ cups (150 g) riced cauliflower**
**¼ cup (56 g) butter, melted, divided**
**¼ cup (60 ml) of your favorite hot sauce, divided**

**Yield: 4 servings**

Bring a pot of lightly salted water to a boil. Peel and rinse the potatoes, and boil for 15 to 20 minutes. At this point, they should still be somewhat firm. Drain and rinse until cool enough to handle.

Shred the potatoes into a bowl using the coarse section of a hand grater.

Add the cauliflower, 2 tablespoons (28 g) of the melted butter, and 2 tablespoons (30 ml) of the hot sauce, and mix until well combined.

Preheat the oven to 425°F (220°C or gas mark 7). Have ready a baking sheet lined with parchment or a silicone baking mat.

Using a very small ice cream scoop (if you don't have one, you can use a measuring spoon or melon baller), create balls of the mixture, about 2 teaspoons to 1 tablespoon (15 g) of mixture, and arrange in a single layer on the baking sheet. If you are a tot purist, you can hand-form these into cylinder shapes.

Bake for 30 minutes, tossing halfway through, until browned and crispy.

While baking, mix together the remaining butter with the remaining hot sauce.

Remove from the oven, and carefully transfer to a bowl. Add the buffalo mixture to the bowl and toss to coat.

Serve hot.

# Garlic Rosemary Fries

French fries are a natural go-to side for burgers. The trick to making crispy-on-the-outside-pillowy-soft-on-the-inside fries is the double fry. Most folks don't realize fries have to be fried—not once, but twice. If you have a deep fryer, now is a perfect time to use it. If not, a heavy pot filled with 4 to 5 inches (10 to 12 cm) of oil will do the trick just fine.

Cut the potatoes into the desired fry shape (wedges, steak fries, skinny, fat, etc.) and place in a bowl of cold water to prevent discoloring. Soak for at least 2 hours, or up to overnight, in the refrigerator. Drain, rinse, and pat completely dry.

Heat oil to 300°F (150°C). Have ready a large bowl lined with paper towels.

Add the fries to the oil (make sure they have enough room to float around freely) and fry for 5 to 7 minutes. This will ensure the fries are cooked all the way through. The fries will be tender at this point, but not browned or crispy.

While the fries are frying, in a small bowl mix together the garlic, rosemary, and salt.

Carefully remove the fries from the oil, using a slotted or strainer spoon, and transfer to the towel-lined bowl to absorb excess oil.

Turn up the heat to 400°F (204°C). Add the fries to the oil and fry until golden and crispy, about 2 minutes. Note that the fries will continue to brown once removed from the oil, so take care not to overcook.

Carefully transfer to the towel-lined bowl. Toss quickly to drain off excess oil. Remove the towels, but leave the fries in the bowl.

While still hot, sprinkle with the seasoning mixture and toss to coat. Serve immediately.

4 large russet potatoes, peeled if desired
Oil, for frying (canola oil is good for fries)
2 tablespoons (20 g) minced garlic
2 tablespoons (11 g) fresh chopped rosemary
½ teaspoon salt

**Yield: 4 servings**

# Cilantro Lime Rice

This is a version of the rice they make at Chipotle Mexican Grill. It's another great side dish to serve up alongside the Mexican-inspired burgers, like South by Southwest Burger on page 84.

2 tablespoons (28 g) butter
1⅓ cups (253 g) uncooked basmati rice
2 cups (470 ml) water
1 teaspoon salt
Juice of 2 limes
¼ cup (4 g) finely chopped fresh cilantro

**Yield: about 3 cups (495 g)**

In a pot with a tight-fitting lid, melt the butter over low heat.

Add the rice, and stir to coat. Cook for about 1 minute to lightly toast the rice.

Add the water, salt, and lime juice. Bring to a boil. Reduce to a simmer and cover.

Simmer, covered, for 20 to 25 minutes, or until the rice is tender and the liquid is absorbed. Stir occasionally to prevent the rice from sticking or scorching on the bottom of the pan.

Fluff with a fork and fold in the chopped cilantro.

# Creamy BBQ Coleslaw

This coleslaw adds a tangy, sassy twist to the classic coleslaw. It tastes great piled onto the Pulled "Pork" Sliders (page 66) or on its own as a side dish.

1 cup (224 g) mayonnaise, store-bought
   or homemade vegan (page 161)
1 cup (80 ml) barbecue sauce,
   store-bought or homemade (page 155
   or 166)
⅓ cup (116 g) agave nectar
2 tablespoons (30 ml) apple cider vinegar
Salt and pepper
1 medium head cabbage, cored and
   shredded

**Yield: 12 servings**

In a large bowl, combine the mayonnaise, barbecue sauce, agave, vinegar, and salt and pepper to taste. Add the cabbage and toss to coat.

Refrigerate until ready to serve.

# Fried Yuca with Gringa Aji Dipping Sauce

Inspired by Peruvian cuisine, but adapted for easier-to-find peppers, this version of Aji Verde might just become one of your new favorite condiments. The fried yuca is very similar to potato fries, but a little bit sweeter. Yuca root—otherwise known as cassava—is brown and rough on the outside, but crisp and white or yellowish on the inside. The thick woody skin is too thick to be peeled with a potato peeler, so you will need to peel it with a knife. If you have a deep fryer, this is a great way to use it. Otherwise, a deep pot filled with about 4 inches (10 cm) of vegetable oil should do just fine.

---

**FOR GRINGA AJI DIPPING SAUCE:**
6 fresh jalapeño peppers
2 ounces (56 g) fresh baby spinach leaves
1 ounce (28 g) fresh parsley
1½ cups (355 ml) mild-flavored
 vegetable oil
2 tablespoons (30 g) minced garlic
 (about 6 cloves)
1 tablespoon (15 ml) lemon juice
Salt and pepper, to taste

**FOR FRIED YUCA:**
1 large yuca root
½ teaspoon ground cumin
½ teaspoon salt
½ teaspoon paprika
½ teaspoon garlic powder
½ teaspoon onion powder
Oil, for frying

**Yield: 4 servings of yuca and 2 cups
 (470 ml) sauce**

**To make the dipping sauce:** Remove the stems from the jalapeños (and seeds, if not using) and place on a lined baking sheet and roast at 350°F (180°C, or gas mark 4) for about 30 minutes.

Add all remaining sauce ingredients to a blender and purée until smooth. Refrigerate until ready to serve.

**To make the fried yuca:** Peel and slice the yuca into fry-size pieces. Rinse under cool water to remove excess starch and prevent discoloring. Steam the fries for about 20 minutes prior to frying. This will soften and precook the fries.

While the yuca is steaming, prepare the spice mixture by adding all the spices to a small container with a tight-fitting lid and shake to mix.

Preheat the oil to 350°F (180°C). Have ready a plate or baking sheet lined with paper towels.

Carefully add the steamed fries in small batches to the oil, being careful not to overcrowd. Allow to cook for about 3 to 5 minutes, remove from the oil, and place on the paper towel–lined tray to absorb excess oil. Sprinkle with the seasoning mixture to taste. Serve hot with the dipping sauce.

# Crispy Fried Onions

Slice those onions as thinly as possible for the crispiest of crispy onions. If you have a deep fryer, this is a good time to use it. If not, a pot filled with about 2 to 3 inches (5 to 7.5 cm) of oil will work just fine.

Combine the lemon juice and milk in a bowl. Set aside for 2 to 3 minutes. It will curdle and become like buttermilk.

Add the thinly sliced onions to the buttermilk mixture and let soak for 5 minutes.

Heat the oil to 375°F (190°C). Have ready a plate lined with paper towels.

Mix together the flour, salt, and pepper in a medium bowl. Add in the sliced onions and toss to coat.

Carefully add the coated onions to the oil, making sure they can float around freely. You may need to do this in several batches. Fry for about 5 minutes, or until golden and crispy all the way through.

Carefully transfer to the towel-lined plate to absorb excess oil. Cool completely before storing in an airtight container.

1 tablespoon (15 ml) lemon juice
1 cup (235 ml) unsweetened nondairy milk or milk of choice
1 large yellow onion, sliced very thin
Oil, for frying
⅔ cup (84 g) all-purpose flour
¼ teaspoon salt
¼ teaspoon pepper

**Yield: varies depending on the size of your onion**

# Baked Onion Rings

Onion rings come in second only to golden delicious french fries as the perfect side to a burger. And while deep-fried is always delicious, this baked version is darned tasty.

Preheat the oven to 450°F (230°C, or gas mark 8). Have ready a baking sheet lined with parchment or a silicone baking mat.

Separate the onion slices into individual rings.

In a small bowl, whisk together the aquafaba and milk. Set aside.

In a separate bowl, combine the panko crumbs and dried parsley. Set aside.

Add the flour, paprika, salt, and black pepper to a large resealable plastic bag or a container with a tight-fitting lid. Add the onion rings, and shake until they are well coated with flour.

Place the flour-coated onion rings into the aquafaba mixture, a few at a time, and toss lightly with tongs until coated.

Transfer to the panko crumbs and toss to coat. Arrange in a single layer on the baking sheet and bake 12 to 15 minutes, or until the crumbs are a light golden brown.

1 medium yellow onion, cut into ¼-inch (6 mm) thick slices
⅓ cup (80 ml) aquafaba (liquid from a can of chickpeas)
¼ cup (60 ml) unsweetened almond or milk of choice
½ cup (40 g) panko-style bread crumbs
1 teaspoon dried parsley
½ cup (62 g) all-purpose flour
¼ teaspoon smoked paprika
¼ teaspoon salt
⅛ teaspoon black pepper

**Yield: 2 to 4 servings**

## 10

# SAUCES, DIPS, BITS, AND BUNS

You know what they say: The sauce makes the meal. A good sauce can bring individual components of a dish into a composed meal. It's the tie that binds it all together. In addition to sauces and dressings, you'll find a few key, basic recipes that are used throughout this book many times, as well as some baked buns for all those delicious burgers.

# Nacho Cheesy Sauce

Perfect to top tortilla chips, tacos, burritos, and even chili.

2 cups (470 ml) plain soy creamer
½ cup (60 g) nutritional yeast
½ cup (65 g) raw cashews
1 tablespoon (16 g) tahini
2 tablespoons (36 g) white miso
2 tablespoons (16 g) cornstarch
1 tablespoon (8 g) onion powder
1 tablespoon (8 g) garlic powder
1 tablespoon (8 g) ground mustard
1 teaspoon ground cumin
1 teaspoon hot sauce, or more to taste
2 to 4 slices jarred or canned jalapeños
1 tablespoon (15 ml) juice from jar
   of jalapeños

**Yield: 2½ cups (590 g)**

Place all the ingredients in a blender or food processor and process until smooth.

Place in a saucepan. Heat over low heat until it thickens, stirring constantly so it doesn't get clumpy or scorch. Store in an airtight container in the refrigerator until ready to use.

# Yogurt Tahini Sauce

This tangy sauce works so well as a spread for many of the burgers in this book, including the Super Quinoa Burger (page 87). It is also delicious as a salad dressing or dip for veggies.

1 container (6 ounces [170 g])
   plain yogurt
3 tablespoons (48 g) tahini
2 tablespoons (30 ml) sesame oil
1 tablespoon (15 ml) lemon juice
½ teaspoon dill
½ teaspoon paprika
Salt and pepper

**Yield: 1 cup (240 g)**

Place all the ingredients in a blender and blend until smooth, or whisk together very well.

Store in an airtight container in the refrigerator until ready to use.

# Strawberry BBQ Sauce

Sweet, smoky, tangy, and a little bit of heat make this unique barbecue sauce the perfect addition to your sauce repertoire.

In a pot, heat the oil over medium-high heat. Add the yellow and red onions and sauté for 3 minutes. Add the garlic and sauté an additional 3 minutes, or until fragrant and translucent. Add in the strawberries, salt, and pepper. Continue to cook for an additional 5 minutes, stirring often.

Stir in the diced tomatoes, tomato sauce, brown sugar, chipotle powder, and chili flakes. Bring to a boil, reduce to a simmer, and simmer uncovered for 30 minutes, returning to stir a few times. Remove from the heat. Using an immersion blender (or carefully transfer to a tabletop blender), blend smooth, if desired.

Store in an airtight container in the refrigerator for up to 2 weeks.

2 tablespoons (28 ml) vegetable oil
½ cup (80 g) diced yellow onion
½ cup (80 g) diced red onion
2 tablespoons (17 g) minced garlic
1 pound (454 g) fresh strawberries, stems removed and cut into quarters
¼ teaspoon salt
¼ teaspoon black pepper
1 can (15 ounces [425 g]) diced tomatoes in juice
8 ounces (227 g) tomato sauce
½ cup (110 g) tightly packed brown sugar
¼ to ½ teaspoon chipotle powder, add more or less to taste
¼ teaspoon red chili flakes, add more or less to taste

**Yield: 3 cups (705 ml)**

# Indian-Spiced Mayo

Here's an aioli-type spread that tastes great on the Middle Eastern–inspired burgers throughout this book.

Combine all the ingredients in an airtight container and keep refrigerated until ready to use.

1 cup (225 g) mayonnaise, store-bought or homemade vegan (page 161)
1 tablespoon (8 g) garam masala
Pinch of paprika
Pinch of turmeric
Salt and pepper, to taste

**Yield: 1 cup (225 g)**

# Pesto (Three Ways)

## Simple Pesto

This vegan pesto is so good, consider doubling the recipe. Use half on a burger and reserve the other half to spread on a toasted bun or throw on some pasta later.

14 large fresh basil leaves
2 or 3 cloves garlic
½ teaspoon coarse sea salt
1 tablespoon (8 g) toasted pine nuts
1 tablespoon (8 g) raw walnut pieces
1 tablespoon (8 g) nutritional yeast
3 tablespoons (45 ml) olive oil

**Yield: 1/2 cup (130 g)**

In a food processor, combine the basil, garlic, salt, pine nuts, walnuts, and nutritional yeast and process until a purée is formed. Drizzle in the oil and pulse a few more times to combine.

## Essential Pesto Sauce with Any Herb or Leafy Greens

This pesto is so fresh and versatile. A small spoonful of miso paste adds the most irresistible savory depth. We most often associate basil with pesto sauce, but in fact, it can be made with any type of greens or fresh herbs. Use this recipe as your template, and substitute in your greens of choice, along with any type of nuts or seeds.

2 cups (96 g) loosely packed herbs or
   leafy greens
2 tablespoons (18 g) toasted nuts
   or seeds
2 tablespoons (10 g) grated Parmesan
   or Pecorino cheese
1 tablespoon (15 ml) freshly squeezed
   lemon juice
1 teaspoon miso paste
1 clove garlic
¼ cup (60 ml) extra-virgin olive oil

**Yield: ½ cup (120 ml)**

Add the herbs or greens, nuts, cheese, lemon juice, miso paste, and garlic to the bowl of a food processor or blender. Pulse until finely chopped. Gradually pour in the olive oil while processing continuously. Store in an airtight container in the refrigerator for up to 5 days.

# Mixed Greens Pepita Pesto

This pesto has so much vibrant flavor. The pumpkin seeds (pepitas) have a "cheesy" flavor that replaces Parmesan cheese perfectly. Substitute pine nuts for the almonds if desired.

In a food processor, place the basil, arugula, garlic, pumpkin seeds, almonds, lemon juice, salt, and pepper. With the food processor running, drizzle in the olive oil through the top. Stop and scrape down the sides and process again to incorporate. Through the top with the food processor running, add the water 1 tablespoon (15 ml) at a time until the desired consistency is reached.

1 cup (about 24 g) packed fresh basil leaves
1 cup (about 20 g) packed arugula
2 cloves garlic, peeled
½ cup (70 g) raw shelled pumpkin seeds (pepitas)
¼ cup (36 g) raw almonds
¼ cup (60 ml) fresh lemon juice
½ teaspoon salt, or to taste
⅛ teaspoon black pepper, or to taste
2 tablespoons (28 ml) extra-virgin olive oil
2–3 tablespoons (28–45 ml) water, to thin

**Yield: 1½ cups (390 g)**

# Sun-Dried Tomato Aioli

This aioli works on almost any of the burgers in this book, and as a sandwich or bagel spread.

2 cloves garlic
¼ cup (28 g) sun-dried tomatoes
    packed in oil
¼ teaspoon paprika
¼ cup (30 g) pine nuts
¾ cup (168 g) mayonnaise, store-bought
    or homemade vegan (page 161)
Salt and pepper

**Yield: just over 1 cup (250 g)**

In a food processor, combine the garlic, tomatoes, and paprika and process until smooth. Transfer to a bowl.

Add the pine nuts, mayonnaise, and salt and pepper to taste. Stir to combine.

Store in an airtight container, in the fridge, until ready to use.

# Garlic Artichoke Spread

This works well as a burger or sandwich spread and as a dip for crackers and veggies.

2 tablespoons (28 ml) plus ¼ cup (60 ml)
    olive oil, divided
1 yellow onion, chopped
2 tablespoons (30 g) minced garlic
½ teaspoon ground cumin
Pinch of salt and freshly cracked pepper
1 can (14 ounces [392 g]) artichoke
    hearts, drained and roughly chopped
½ cup (60 g) pine nuts (optional)

**Yield: just under 3 cups (685 g)**

Preheat the 2 tablespoons (30 ml) oil over medium-high heat in a flat-bottomed skillet.

Add the onion, garlic, cumin, salt, and pepper. Sauté until translucent and fragrant and the edges of the onions just start to turn brown, 5 to 7 minutes.

Transfer to a blender or food processor, add the artichoke hearts and remaining ¼ cup (60 ml) oil, and blend until smooth.

Transfer to a bowl and mix in the pine nuts.

# Aioli Dipping Sauce

This basic aioli can be your inspiration to never again be tempted to use plain old mayo—unless, of course, you love plain old mayo.

In small bowl, stir together the mayonnaise, sour cream, olive oil, and lemon juice.

Stir in the basil, chives, garlic, lemon zest, salt, and pepper.

Cover and refrigerate for at least 30 minutes, or until ready to use.

⅔ cup (150 g) mayonnaise, store-bought or homemade vegan (page 161)

⅓ cup (80 g) sour cream, store-bought or homemade nondairy (page 162)

2 tablespoons (28 ml) extra-virgin olive oil

1½ tablespoons (23 ml) fresh lemon juice

3 tablespoons (9 g) chopped fresh basil

2 tablespoons (12 g) chopped fresh chives

1 tablespoon (15 g) minced garlic

1 tablespoon (8 g) lemon zest

½ teaspoon sea salt

½ teaspoon freshly cracked pepper

**Yield: 1½ cups (338 g)**

# Creamy Balsamic Dressing

This creamy dressing is not only a great basic dressing—but it's divine schmeared on sandwiches.

Place all the ingredients in a blender and process until smooth.

Keep refrigerated in an airtight container until ready to use. Lasts about 1 week.

12 ounces (340 g) extra-firm tofu, drained but not pressed

½ cup (120 ml) olive oil

¼ cup (60 ml) balsamic vinegar

1 tablespoon (8 g) garlic powder

1 tablespoon (8 g) onion powder

Salt and pepper, to taste

**Yield: 1½ cups (375 g)**

# Vegan Mayonnaise (Two Ways)

## Easy Tofu Cashew Mayo

Here are two different methods for preparing vegan mayo. Try them both.

Place the tofu, cashews, lemon juice, sugar, mustard, vinegar, and salt in a blender or food processor and process until smooth.

Slowly drizzle in the oil and pulse until you get the consistency that you like.

Store in an airtight container in the refrigerator for up to 2 weeks.

7 ounces (195 g) extra-firm tofu, drained and pressed
¼ cup (35 g) raw cashews, ground into a very fine powder
1 tablespoon (15 ml) lemon juice
1 tablespoon (12 g) raw sugar or (21 g) agave nectar
1½ teaspoons brown or Dijon mustard
1 teaspoon apple cider or rice wine vinegar
½ teaspoon sea salt
6 tablespoons (90 ml) canola oil

**Yield: almost 2 cups (450 g)**

## Aquafaba Mayo

Add the aquafaba, juice or vinegar, mustard seed, salt, and sugar* to the cup of your immersion blender. If your immersion blender did not come with a cup, a wide-mouthed glass jar will work. Make sure to use a tall, slender container for this. A regular bowl will not work. Blend until white and foamy, about 15 seconds.

Slowly drizzle in the oil in a very thin stream, a small amount at a time, while constantly blending. Allow the oil to completely incorporate before adding more. DO NOT STOP THE BLENDER DURING THE ENTIRE PROCESS! Continue to add oil until it is all incorporated. This process should take up to 5 full minutes. Be patient. Be *very, very* patient. Upon adding the last of the oil, it should be thick and silky … just like mayo. Keep refrigerated in an airtight container until ready to use. Should last up to 2 weeks. Use as is as mayo or add more seasonings to make a variety of aiolis, spreads, and sauces.

¼ cup (60 ml) liquid from a can of garbanzo beans (a.k.a. aquafaba), room temperature
2 teaspoons lemon juice, lime juice, or apple cider vinegar (your choice)
½ teaspoon dried ground mustard seed
¼ teaspoon salt
¼ teaspoon sugar*
¾ cup (180 ml) mild-flavored vegetable oil
*If you prefer to use a liquid sweetener, such as agave or date syrup, do not add until after the mayo has emulsified and thickened. Simply stir it in afterward.

**Yield: 1 cup (235 ml)**

# Nondairy Sour Cream

Although nondairy versions of traditional dairy products are becoming more readily available, you might occasionally need to whip up a delicious batch of your own.

7 ounces (195 g) extra-firm tofu, drained well and pressed
¼ cup (28 g) raw cashews, ground into a fine powder
1 tablespoon (15 ml) white rice vinegar
1 tablespoon (15 ml) lemon or lime juice
1 tablespoon (18 g) white miso
1 tablespoon (15 ml) mild-flavored vegetable oil

**Yield: about 1½ cups (345 g)**

Place all the ingredients in a blender or food processor and process until very, very smooth and creamy. Keep refrigerated in an airtight container until ready to use. Should last up to 1 week.

# Sweet Mustard Sauce

This innocent sauce offers a bit of sweet relief when slathered onto some of the more spicy burgers in this book.

½ cup (120 g) mayonnaise, store-bought or homemade vegan (page 161)
2 tablespoons (42 g) agave nectar
2 tablespoons (30 g) Dijon mustard
1 tablespoon (6 g) finely diced chives
Salt and pepper

**Yield: ¾ cup (190 g)**

Whisk together all the ingredients.
Store in an airtight container in the refrigerator until ready to use.

# Tzatziki Sauce

Fresh and tangy, this sauce works well with falafel, in a pita sandwich, or as a dip for warm pita triangles or flatbread. It is also great on the Three Lentil Burger (page 76).

Strain the excess liquid from the yogurt by pouring the yogurt into the center of several folded layers of cheesecloth, tying it off, and suspending it over a bowl. Use the handle of a wooden spoon to tie the cheesecloth to and then rest each end of the spoon over the edge of a mixing bowl. Let sit for a few hours.

In a bowl, combine the strained yogurt, cucumber, dill, garlic, lemon juice, oil, and salt and pepper to taste.

Keep refrigerated in an airtight container until ready to use. This should keep for about 1 week.

12 ounces (340 g) unsweetened plain yogurt
1½ cups (200 g) seeded and finely diced cucumber
1 tablespoon (3 g) fresh dill
1 tablespoon (15 g) minced garlic
1 tablespoon (15 ml) lemon juice
1 tablespoon (15 ml) olive oil
Salt and pepper

**Yield: just over 2 cups (480 g)**

# Mango Salsa

Just try not to eat this awesome salsa for breakfast, lunch, dinner, and everything in between.

In a bowl, combine all the ingredients and refrigerate overnight to enhance the flavor.

Serve with tortilla chips, or pile on top of some of the spicier burgers for a nice contrast in flavor and texture.

1 mango, peeled, seeded, and diced
½ cup (8 g) finely chopped fresh cilantro
½ cup (80 g) finely diced red onion
1 teaspoon garlic powder
½ teaspoon salt, or more to taste
½ teaspoon black pepper
1 serrano chile, seeded, cored, and finely diced

**Yield: about 1½ cups (375 g)**

# Creamy Sesame Sriracha Sauce

A.K.A. Spicy Sushi Sauce, this salmon-colored sauce is an absolute favorite sauce. Go ahead: put it on everything.

12 ounces (340 g) soft silken tofu
¾ cup (180 ml) mild-flavored
    vegetable oil
¼ cup (60 ml) sesame oil
3 tablespoons (45 ml) sriracha sauce
2 tablespoons (30 ml) rice vinegar
1 tablespoon (10 g) minced garlic
½ teaspoon ground mustard seed
½ teaspoon salt

**Yield: about 2 cups (470 ml)**

Add all the ingredients to a blender and blend until silky smooth. Keep stored in an airtight container in the refrigerator. This will keep for at least 2 weeks.

# Creamy Cumin Ranch Dressing

Here's a creamy, tangy, herby, dairy-free ranch dressing with a hint of southwest flavors. Try it on salads, burgers, baked potatoes, stirred into soup, as a dip for raw veggies or French fries ... the possibilities are endless!

¾ cup (105 g) raw cashews (soaked for
    1–2 hours if you don't have a
    high-speed blender, then drained)
½ cup (120 ml) water, plus more to thin
    if needed
Juice of 1 lemon
1 tablespoon (15 ml) apple cider vinegar
1 clove garlic
1 teaspoon ground cumin
1 teaspoon dried dill
1 teaspoon snipped chives
½ teaspoon smoked paprika
½ teaspoon onion powder
½ teaspoon dried oregano
½ teaspoon salt, or to taste

**Yield: about 1¼ cups (295 ml)**

Blend all the ingredients in a high-speed blender until smooth. Add more water 1 tablespoon (15 ml) at a time, if necessary, to thin.

# BEST Guacamole

Guacamole is life. Just a few simple ingredients bring so much flavor and texture. It's creamy, yet chunky, tangy, and spicy. Make it and put it on everything!

In a medium bowl, mash the avocado with a fork or potato masher until smooth.

Add all the other ingredients and use 2 jalapeños if you like spicy! Stir to combine. Taste and adjust the seasoning, if necessary.

Serve immediately.

4 avocados, pits and peels removed
1 Roma tomato, diced
2–3 tablespoons (20–30 g) diced
    red onion
¼ cup (4 g) cilantro, chopped
Juice of 1 lime
Salt
1–2 jalapeños, ribs and seeds removed,
    diced

**Yield: about 3 cups (675 g)**

# Basic Everyday Vinaigrette

Every home cook should have a basic vinaigrette recipe in their arsenal, for Buddha bowls and beyond. To get the most out of this much-loved, tried-and-true version, approach it as a flexible template rather than a set recipe. Experiment with different vinegars, lemon, or other types of citrus juice to vary the flavor profile of your vinaigrette.

Combine all the ingredients in a small jar. Shake well until the dressing is emulsified. Use immediately or store in the refrigerator in an airtight container until ready to serve (up to 5 days).

⅓ cup (80 ml) freshly squeezed lemon
    juice or vinegar, such as balsamic,
    apple cider, white wine, red wine, or
    rice vinegar
1 tablespoon (11 g) Dijon mustard
1 clove garlic, minced
⅓ cup (80 ml) extra-virgin olive oil
½ teaspoon kosher salt
¼ teaspoon freshly ground black pepper

**Yield: about ¾ cup (180 ml)**

**VARIATIONS**
- **Herb Vinaigrette:** Add 2 tablespoons (30 ml) white balsamic vinegar and 2 tablespoons (6 g) finely chopped herbs.
- **White Wine-Lemon Vinaigrette:** Add ¼ cup (12 g) loosely packed fresh herbs (cilantro, basil, mint, dill).

# Quick and Easy Marinara Sauce

This marinara recipe tastes like a sauce you'd get in a restaurant, yet it's so easy to make and is ready in just twenty minutes! This recipe makes a lot because it goes well with so many different dishes. Cook once, eat twice (or more)! Use it on pasta and pizza or as a dip for quesadillas or garlic bread. Add it to soup, rice, or stuffed peppers. Leftovers will keep in the fridge for several days and in the freezer for up to 6 months, but feel free to halve the recipe if you wish.

1 can (28 ounces, or 785 g) crushed
    tomatoes
1 can (15 ounces, or 425 g) tomato sauce
¼ cup (64 g) tomato paste
1 teaspoon salt, or to taste
1 teaspoon dried basil
1 teaspoon dried oregano
½ teaspoon garlic powder
½ teaspoon onion powder
1 teaspoon granulated organic
    white sugar

**Yield: 5 cups (1.2 L)**

Add all the ingredients to a pot over medium heat on the stove. When it begins to bubble, turn the heat down to low and simmer for 15 to 20 minutes. Add more salt or seasonings to taste, if necessary.

**Tip:** To make the sauce on the chunkier side, used diced tomatoes instead of the crushed.

# Sweet-and-Spicy BBQ Sauce

A little sweet and a little heat balance perfectly in this easy blender sauce. It will make you want to slather everything in BBQ sauce.

6 ounces (170 g) tomato paste
¼ cup (60 ml) apple cider vinegar
¼ cup (60 ml) balsamic vinegar
3 tablespoons (60 g) pure maple syrup
1–2 chipotle peppers in adobo
1 teaspoon smoked paprika
1 teaspoon ground mustard
½ teaspoon onion powder
¼ teaspoon garlic powder
½ teaspoon salt, or to taste
½ cup (120 ml) water, to thin, or more
    as needed

**Yield: 1½ cups (355 ml)**

Place all the ingredients in a blender; use 2 chipotle peppers if you like it spicier. Purée until smooth.

Transfer the sauce to a pot over medium-high heat and bring to a boil and then reduce the heat to low. Simmer for 15 to 20 minutes until thick, or until the desired consistency is reached.

# Romesco Sauce

This sauce is thick like a pesto but made with peppers. Many versions are thickened with leftover bread, but this one uses panko bread crumbs because they're a pantry staple and they help create that wonderful pesto-like texture. This version is smoky and a little sweet, and it pairs well with a variety of dishes. Try it on pasta or rice. Use it as a dip for garlic bread or quesadillas or simply drizzle it over roasted vegetables.

---

Place all the ingredients in a food processor. Process until mostly smooth. It should resemble a pesto in texture, so it won't be totally smooth.

1 jar (12 ounces, or 340 g) roasted red peppers, drained

1 can (15 ounces, or 425 g) fired-roasted diced tomatoes, drained

½ cup (73 g) raw almonds

¼ cup (13 g) panko bread crumbs or regular bread crumbs

2 cloves garlic

1 tablespoon (7 g) smoked paprika

½ teaspoon salt, or to taste

1 tablespoon (15 ml) balsamic vinegar

**Yield: about 3 cups (700 ml)**

# Sharp Salsa Queso Dip

This may seem like an odd mix of ingredients, but you are going to LOVE this dip. It tastes like sharp pub cheese, but with a salsa twist. You won't believe it doesn't contain cheese.

---

In a food processor, pulse the cashews until they resemble a fine crumb. Add the tahini, miso, and salt and pulse to combine. Add the salsa and purée until mostly smooth. If you'd like to thin it out, add water 1 tablespoon (15 ml) at a time until the desired consistency is reached.

1 cup (140 g) raw cashews

¼ cup (60 g) tahini

3 tablespoons (48 g) mellow white miso paste

¾ teaspoon salt

1 cup (260 g) spicy salsa (see Tip)

Water to thin as needed

**Yield: 2 cups (about 500 g)**

**Tip:** Now is not the time for mild salsa. The other ingredients will mellow out the heat, so go with a medium to spicy one. A fairly runny salsa works best, but if you use a chunkier one, add water to thin as needed.

# Butternut Mac Cheese Sauce

Made with real whole-food ingredients, this sauce shockingly resembles dairy cheese sauce. It's beloved by everyone from vegans to carnivores and kids to adults. Try it with pasta for a delicious creamy mac and cheese, over baked potatoes, stirred into soup, or as a dip for raw or steamed vegetables.

1½ cups (210 g) peeled and chopped
    butternut squash
½ sweet onion, diced
¼ cup (35 g) raw cashews
1 tablespoon (15 ml) fresh lemon juice
1 teaspoon salt
¼ teaspoon garlic powder
¼ teaspoon black pepper
¼ teaspoon mustard powder
⅛ teaspoon smoked paprika
⅛ teaspoon turmeric
⅛ teaspoon ground nutmeg

**Yield: 2 cups (475 ml)**

Add the butternut squash, onion, and cashews to a pot over high heat and cover with water by at least 1 to 2 inches (2.5 to 5 cm). Bring to a boil and then reduce the heat to low. Simmer for 15 to 20 minutes until the squash is fork-tender. Reserve ¼ cup (60 ml) of the cooking liquid and drain the rest.

Add the squash mixture to a high-speed blender along with the reserved cooking liquid and the remaining ingredients. Blend until smooth.

# Avocado Green Goddess Dressing

Green Goddess dressing is a cool and creamy, herb and garlic sauce conceived in San Francisco in the 1920s, with a popular resurgence in the '70s and '80s. Here, it gets a healthy, fresh spin by putting lush avocado and Greek yogurt at the forefront for an incredibly creamy dressing, packed with good fats to help make any Buddha bowl or salad more satisfying and filling.

Combine the avocado, yogurt, herbs, garlic, oil, vinegar, lemon juice, salt, and pepper in the bowl of a food processor. Blend continuously until smooth and well combined, scraping down the sides of the bowl as necessary. With the food processor running, add the water, 1 tablespoon (15 ml) at a time, until it reaches the desired consistency. Store in an airtight container in the refrigerator for up to 3 days.

1 medium ripe avocado
¼ cup (60 g) plain Greek yogurt
3 tablespoons (9 g) packed snipped chives
3 tablespoons (9 g) packed fresh basil
3 tablespoons (9 g) packed fresh parsley
1 clove garlic
2 tablespoons (28 ml) avocado oil or extra-virgin olive oil
2 tablespoons (30 ml) apple cider vinegar
2 tablespoons (30 ml) freshly squeezed lemon juice
½ teaspoon kosher salt
¼ teaspoon freshly ground black pepper
5 tablespoons (75 ml) water

**Yield: about ¾ cup (180 ml)**

# Chimichurri Sauce

Chimichurri, the vibrant green sauce that hails from Argentina, is an herb lover's dream come true. With nearly a bundle of herbs plus a splash of lemon and vinegar, it is bright and bold, with a fresh tang that livens up everything it touches.

Add the herbs, garlic, and salt to the bowl of a food processor. Pulse in 2-second bursts until the herbs are finely chopped. Scrape down the sides of the bowl. With the motor running, slowly pour in the oil, lemon juice, and vinegar, and process until well combined, about 1 minute. Store in an airtight container in the refrigerator for up to 4 days.

1 packed cup (16 g) cilantro leaves
½ packed cup (24 g) parsley leaves
1 clove garlic
½ teaspoon kosher salt
⅓ cup (80 ml) extra-virgin olive oil
2 tablespoons (30 ml) freshly squeezed lemon juice
1 tablespoon (15 ml) red wine vinegar

**Yield: about ¾ cup (180 ml)**

# Avocado Sauce

Calling all avocado lovers! If avocado is a regular addition to your Buddha bowls or salads, here's how to turn your favorite produce into a rich and creamy, pourable sauce that goes with everything. This sauce comes together in minutes and is a great way to use up overripe avocados that are on their last leg, though firm avocados will benefit from an extra couple of days to soften. Give it some extra flair with a spoonful of tangy Greek yogurt or a handful of herbs.

---

**1 ripe avocado, peeled and pitted**
**½ cup (120 ml) water**
**Juice from 1 lemon or lime**
**1 clove garlic**
**¼ teaspoon kosher salt**
**¼ teaspoon freshly ground black pepper**

**Yield: about 1 cup (235 ml)**

Place the ingredients in the bowl of a food processor or blender. Process continuously until well combined and smooth, about 1 minute. Store in an airtight container in the refrigerator for up to 3 days.

**VARIATIONS**
- **Avocado-Yogurt Sauce:** Add 2 tablespoons (30 g) Greek yogurt.
- **Herbed Avocado Sauce:** Add ¼ cup (12 g) loosely packed fresh herbs (cilantro, basil, mint, dill).

# Maple Dijon Vinaigrette

Don't buy pricey store-bought vinaigrettes with questionable ingredients. This sweet and tangy dressing is incredibly easy to make, and it is made from pantry staples. It will become a staple in your fridge, too.

---

**3 tablespoons (45 g) Dijon mustard**
**2 tablespoons (40 g) pure maple syrup, or to taste**
**2 tablespoons (28 ml) apple cider vinegar**
**½ teaspoon salt, or to taste**
**½ cup (120 ml) extra-virgin olive oil**

**Yield: about 1 cup (235 ml)**

In a small bowl, whisk together all the ingredients until smooth.

# Creamy Feta Sauce

If you have a thing for briny feta cheese, you are going to love this sauce. It's blended together with a few basic kitchen staples for a super easy, creamy sauce to be drizzled over everything. Give it a simple twist with a handful of your favorite herbs or a roasted red pepper for a pop of color and hint of smokiness.

Place all the ingredients in the bowl of a food processor or blender. Process continuously until the sauce is smooth, 1 to 2 minutes. Thin with additional water, as desired.

Serve immediately or store in a covered container in the refrigerator until ready to use (up to 4 days).

4 ounces (115 g) crumbled feta, at room temperature
3 tablespoons (45 ml) water
1 tablespoon (15 ml) extra-virgin olive oil
½ teaspoon kosher salt

**Yield: about ½ cup (120 ml)**

**VARIATIONS**
- **Herbed Feta Sauce:** Add ¼ cup (12 g) finely chopped fresh herbs (basil, cilantro, dill, mint, parsley, tarragon).
- **Roasted Red Pepper and Feta Sauce:** Add 1 roasted red pepper.

# Light and Creamy Goat Cheese Sauce

If you're feeling a little indulgent, get out your food processor and nubby log of soft goat cheese from the fridge, and in a matter of minutes you'll have a tangy and creamy sauce to drizzle over Buddha bowls or salads. Buy good-quality ingredients, especially when they are the shining stars in a recipe, as the cheese is here.

Place all the ingredients in the bowl of a food processor or blender. Process continuously until the sauce is smooth, 1 to 2 minutes. Store in an airtight container in the refrigerator for up to 4 days.

4 ounces (115 g) goat cheese, at room temperature
1 tablespoon (15 ml) extra-virgin olive oil
2 tablespoons (30 ml) water
½ teaspoon kosher salt

**Yield: about ½ cup (120 ml)**

**VARIATION**
- **Herbed Goat Cheese Sauce:** Add ¼ cup (12 g) chopped fresh herbs (basil, dill, mint, chives, tarragon).

# Miso-Ginger Sauce

Miso paste should be one of your most-used condiments, particularly white miso. It's an ultra-savory, umami-rich ingredient made primarily from fermented soybeans, and even just a small spoonful can bring a dish to life. Here, it's blended with cashews and a generous amount of fresh ginger for a full-flavored, creamy sauce.

¼ cup (36 g) raw unsalted cashews,
    soaked in water overnight and drained
¼ cup (60 ml) rice vinegar
2 tablespoons (30 g) white miso paste
2 tablespoons (30 ml) water
1 tablespoon (6 g) chopped fresh ginger
1½ teaspoons toasted sesame oil
1 teaspoon honey
1 clove garlic, chopped
Freshly ground black pepper

**Yield: about ¾ cup (180 ml)**

Place all the ingredients in the bowl of a food processor or blender. Process continuously until the sauce is smooth, 2 to 3 minutes. Thin with additional water, as desired.

Serve immediately or store in an airtight container in the refrigerator until ready to use (up to 4 days).

# Peanut Sauce

This peanut sauce gives you the most bang for your buck. With just a handful of basic ingredients, it's quick and easy to pull together at a moment's notice, with pops of earthy, savory, and tangy flavors that make it anything but dull. There's also the option to jazz up basic peanut sauce with a few spoonfuls of sriracha for a spicy punch, red curry paste for a hint of warm, aromatic heat, or chopped scallions for a burst of color.

½ cup (130 g) creamy peanut butter
3 tablespoons (45 ml) soy sauce
2 tablespoons (30 ml) rice vinegar
3 tablespoons (45 ml) water
2 teaspoons toasted sesame oil
1 tablespoon (6 g) finely grated
    fresh ginger
¼ teaspoon cayenne pepper (optional)

**Yield: about 1 cup (235 ml)**

Combine all the ingredients in the bowl of a food processor or blender. Process continuously until smooth and well combined, about 2 minutes.

Serve immediately or store in a covered container in the refrigerator until ready to use (up to 4 days).

**VARIATIONS**
· **Curried Peanut Sauce:** Add 1 teaspoon red curry paste.
· **Spicy Peanut Sauce:** Add 1 to 2 tablespoons (15 to 30 ml) sriracha.
· **Scallion Peanut Sauce:** Add 1 or 2 chopped scallions.

# Raita

Raita is a cool, creamy Indian yogurt sauce, and this version is stirred together with cucumber, fresh herbs, and warm spices, like coriander and garam masala. It's a thick sauce you'll enjoy for taming spicy Buddha bowl ingredients, complementing roasted vegetables, or drizzling onto falafel.

Add the yogurt, cucumber, cilantro (or mint), lemon juice, spices, and salt to a small bowl. Mix together until well combined. Store in an airtight container in the refrigerator for up to 3 days.

1 cup (240 g) plain yogurt
¾ cup (90 g) shredded cucumber
2 tablespoons finely chopped cilantro
   (2 g) or mint (6 g)
1 teaspoon freshly squeezed lemon juice
½ teaspoon ground coriander
½ teaspoon ground garam masala
¼ teaspoon kosher salt

**Yield: about 1 cup (235 ml)**

# Roasted Red Pepper Sauce

If you are guilty of buying a jar of roasted red peppers with grand plans to use them in a new recipe, here's your chance at redemption. Whirl them into this subtly textured, smoky sauce. It's creamy and rich, almost decadent, yet totally healthy and surprisingly easy to pull together in just minutes.

Add all of the ingredients to the bowl of a food processor or blender. Process continuously until well blended and mostly smooth, 2 to 3 minutes. Store in an airtight container in the refrigerator for up to 5 days.

1 jar (12 ounces, or 340 g) roasted red
   peppers, drained
¼ cup (36 g) unsalted toasted almonds
1 clove garlic
¼ cup (60 ml) extra-virgin olive oil
Juice from ½ lemon
1 teaspoon paprika
Kosher salt and freshly ground pepper

**Yield: just over 1 cup (235 ml)**

# Tahini Sauce

This is the sauce that's used more than any other for drizzling over Buddha bowls. It's wildly versatile and has a rich, earthy, and nutty taste that has a knack for pairing well with everything. Try it on roasted vegetables, falafel, tacos, lentils, and rice, anything! Get creative and change it up with the suggested variations below.

⅓ cup (80 g) tahini
⅓ cup (80 ml) water
2 tablespoons (30 ml) freshly squeezed lemon juice
1 clove garlic, minced
½ teaspoon kosher salt
¼ teaspoon freshly ground black pepper

**Yield: about ¾ cup (180 ml)**

Place all the ingredients in the bowl of a food processor or blender. Process continuously until well combined, 1 to 2 minutes. Thin with additional water, if desired. Store in an airtight container in the refrigerator for up to 5 days.

**VARIATIONS**

- **Citrus Tahini Sauce:** Use ¼ cup (60 ml) freshly squeezed lemon juice, 2 tablespoons (28 ml) apple cider vinegar, and 1-2 tablespoons (15-30 ml) water.
- **Dill Tahini Sauce:** Add ¼ cup (12 g) finely chopped fresh dill.
- **Green Tahini Sauce:** Add ¼ cup (12 g) fresh parsley leaves, 2 tablespoons (2 g) fresh cilantro leaves, and 2 tablespoons (6 g) fresh dill.
- **Lemon Tahini Sauce:** Use ¼ cup (60 ml) freshly squeezed lemon juice and 2 tablespoons (30 ml) water.
- **Spicy Maple Tahini Sauce:** Swap freshly squeezed lemon juice for white wine vinegar, and add 1 tablespoon (15 ml) maple syrup and ¼ teaspoon cayenne pepper.
- **Miso Tahini Sauce:** Add 2 teaspoons miso paste.
- **Spicy Tahini Sauce:** Add 1 teaspoon harissa.
- **Tangy Tahini Sauce:** Swap lemon juice for an equal amount of apple cider vinegar.

# Yogurt Sauce

This creamy yogurt sauce is a healthy finishing touch for any Buddha bowl, yet it always feels like something of a treat, most notably when it's doctored up with lemon juice and herbs for a play on ranch dressing. Though Greek yogurt is recommended for its thick texture and tangy flavor, and of course, the extra boost of protein, it's worth noting that any type of plain yogurt will work just fine.

Place the ingredients in a medium mixing bowl, and whisk until well combined. Store in an airtight container in the refrigerator for up to 4 days.

1 cup (240 g) plain Greek yogurt
¼ cup (60 ml) water
1 tablespoon (15 ml) extra-virgin olive oil
1 clove garlic, minced
Kosher salt and freshly ground
    black pepper

**Yield: about 1 cup (235 ml)**

**VARIATIONS**
- **Herb Yogurt Sauce:** Add ¼ cup (12 g) finely chopped fresh herbs (basil, cilantro, dill, mint, parsley, tarragon).
- **Lemon Yogurt Sauce:** Swap the water with freshly squeezed lemon juice.
- **Spicy Yogurt Sauce:** Add 1 to 2 tablespoons (15 to 30 ml) sriracha.
- **Yogurt Ranch Sauce:** Use half water and half freshly squeezed lemon juice, and add 2 tablespoons (6 g) finely chopped parsley and 2 tablespoons (6 g) snipped chives.
- **Harissa Yogurt Sauce:** Add 1 tablespoon (6 g) harissa.

# Chipotle Dipping Sauce

The spiciness of this sauce plays off the sweetness of many recipes, especially the Baked Sweet Potato Fries (page 143). This sauce also works well as a spread for sandwiches, or even on the bun under your burger.

Place all the ingredients in a bowl and mix well.

Keep refrigerated until ready to use. The longer you refrigerate it, the more the chipotle flavor will develop.

1 cup (240 g) sour cream, store-bought
    or homemade nondairy (page 162)
½ teaspoon chipotle powder
½ teaspoon garlic powder
¼ teaspoon dillweed
Salt and pepper, to taste

**Yield: 1 cup (240 g)**

# Taco Seasoning

Sure, it's easy to just buy a pack of taco seasoning at the store, but double check the ingredients to make sure it doesn't have any whey. Store-bought varieties also often contain additional ingredients such as anticaking agents and preservatives. To avoid this, you can make your own by mixing together the following ingredients and storing it in an airtight container.

1 tablespoon (8 g) garlic powder
1 tablespoon (8 g) onion powder
1 tablespoon (13 g) sugar
1 tablespoon (7 g) ground cumin
1 tablespoon (7 g) paprika
2 tablespoons (16 g) chili powder
1½ teaspoons salt

**Yield: ½ cup (128 g)**

Place all the ingredients in a small airtight container and shake vigorously. Two tablespoons (16 g) of this mix roughly equals one packet of store-bought taco seasoning.

# Imitation Bacon Bits

Of course, buying a jar of Bac-Os is still the easiest, but if you are a smidge adventurous, try this.

2 tablespoons (30 ml) liquid smoke
1 scant cup (225 ml) water
1 cup (96 g) TVP granules
¼ teaspoon salt
A few drops red food coloring (optional)
3 tablespoons (45 ml) canola or other
    vegetable oil

**Yield: about 1 cup (100 g)**

To a measuring cup, add the liquid smoke, then fill with the water to get 1 cup (235 ml). In a microwave-safe dish, combine the liquid smoke mixture, TVP granules, salt, and red food coloring, if using. Cover tightly with plastic wrap and microwave for 5 to 6 minutes. Alternatively, bring the water to a boil, pour over the TVP granules mixed with the salt, mix in the liquid smoke and red food coloring, cover, and let sit for 10 minutes.

Preheat a frying pan with the oil. Add the reconstituted TVP to the pan and toss to make sure it all gets coated with oil. Panfry until desired crispness is reached. Stir often. You don't necessarily want to brown them, but rather dry them out, about 10 minutes.

Allow to cool completely before transferring to an airtight container. Store in the refrigerator. Should last at least a week, but probably much longer.

# Bacon Strips

Seriously, folks, just about any vegetable can be turned into bacon. Eggplants, carrots, parsnips, mushrooms, even zucchini. What you're after is smoky, salty, fatty, and a little hint of sweet flavor. So feast on veggie bacon! This marinade will work on just about any veggie with similar results.

Mix together all the ingredients except the vegetables to make a marinade.

Add the sliced vegetables to a resealable plastic bag, or a shallow dish with a lid, and add enough marinade to cover completely. Allow to soak in the marinade for at least 1 hour.

Preheat the oven to 350°F (180°C, or gas mark 4). Line a rimmed baking sheet with parchment, and arrange the marinated vegetables, along with any additional marinade, in a single layer.

Bake for 60 minutes, flipping halfway through. (Note: Some vegetables have a higher water content than others and will take a longer time to cook.)

The vegetables should have absorbed the liquid and browned. They should be crisp around the edges, but soft and chewy in the centers.

Remove from the oven and allow to cool completely before storing in the refrigerator until ready to use.

If a crispier strip is desired, you can panfry on medium-high heat in a bit of oil, until desired crispness is reached.

2 tablespoons (30 ml) liquid smoke
2 tablespoons (30 ml) soy sauce
    or tamari
2 tablespoons (28 ml) mild-flavored
    vegetable oil
1 tablespoon (14 g) tightly packed
    brown sugar
2 teaspoons apple cider vinegar
½ teaspoon onion powder
½ teaspoon garlic powder
½ teaspoon black pepper
¼ teaspoon paprika
¼ cup (60 ml) maple syrup
1 pound (454 g) sliced vegetables, cut
    no more than ¼-inch (6 mm) thick

**Yield: will vary depending on amount
    and type of vegetables used**

# Quick Pickled Red Onions

These pickled red onions are an easy way to add a burst of flavor to any dish. They're sweet and tangy, and they're the perfect complement to so many recipes. Use them to top sandwiches, burgers, salads, tacos, Buddha bowls, and so much more.

**1 large red onion, halved and sliced**
**½ cup (120 ml) white vinegar**
**½ cup (120 ml) water**
**2 teaspoons organic white sugar**
**1 teaspoon sea salt**

**Yield: about 2 cups (340 g)**

Place the onion slices in a glass jar just large enough to hold them.

Heat the white vinegar, water, sugar, and salt over medium-high heat. Bring to a simmer and whisk until the sugar and salt are completely dissolved. This should only take a few minutes. Carefully, pour the mixture over the onions. Press the onions down into the liquid if they are sticking up. Set aside to cool.

Pickled onions will be ready to eat in about 30 minutes. The flavors will get stronger as they sit. Cover tightly and store in the refrigerator for about 1 week.

# Traditional Boiled Seitan

This plain and simple seitan has a neutral beefy flavor and works well in recipes calling for prepared seitan.

**To make the broth:** Combine all the broth ingredients in a large stockpot and bring to a simmer.

**To make the seitan dough:** In a large mixing bowl, combine the flours, then slowly add the water and form into a stiff dough. Knead the dough about 70 times. You can do it right in the bowl. Let rest for 20 minutes.

After resting, take the dough, in the bowl, to the sink and cover with water. Knead the dough until the water becomes milky, then drain off the water and repeat. Do this 10 to 12 times. By the tenth or twelfth time, the dough will feel and look loose and goopy, but the water will still be a little milky.

After the last rinse, add the parsley, scallions, garlic powder, onion powder, and pepper. Mix thoroughly by hand.

Divide the dough in half. Place 1 piece of dough in the center of a large piece of cheesecloth and roll tightly into a log shape. Tie the ends to secure. Repeat with the other piece.

Place both logs in the broth and simmer for 90 minutes.

Remove from the broth and set on a plate to cool. Unwrap. If the cheesecloth is sticking, run under some water, and it should come off easily.

You can store the seitan in the refrigerator wrapped in foil or in a plastic container. To keep it really moist, place some of the broth in the container. Will keep in the fridge for about 2 weeks, or indefinitely in the freezer.

**FOR BOILING BROTH:**
10 cups (2.35 L) water
2 cups (470 ml) soy sauce
10 cloves garlic, chopped in half
5 whole bay leaves
3 slices (2 inches [5 cm] each) fresh ginger or 1 hand, chopped into chunks

**FOR SEITAN DOUGH:**
1 cup (144 g) vital wheat gluten flour
5 cups (600 g) whole wheat flour
2½ cups (588 ml) water
½ cup (32 g) chopped fresh parsley
3 scallions, whites only, finely chopped
1 teaspoon garlic powder
1 teaspoon onion powder
1 to 3 teaspoons freshly cracked pepper, to taste

**Yield: about 4 pounds (1816 g)**

# Addictive Tofu (Two Ways)

Tofu done right is downright addictive! Oven-baked is great because it's mostly hands off, but if you want truly crispy exteriors, panfried is the way to go!

**FOR CRISPY PANFRIED TOFU:**

1 package (14 ounces, or 390 g)
  extra-firm or super-firm tofu (not
  silken), drained
2 tablespoons (28 ml) peanut oil or
  other high-heat oil (such as coconut
  or avocado), divided
Salt and black pepper

**FOR CHEWY OVEN-BAKED TOFU:**

1 package (14 ounces, or 390 g)
  extra-firm or super-firm tofu (not
  silken), drained
2 tablespoons (28 ml) tamari, coconut
  aminos, or soy sauce
1 tablespoon (15 ml) apple cider vinegar
1 tablespoon (15 ml) olive oil
1 tablespoon (20 g) pure maple syrup
1 tablespoon (15 g) Dijon mustard
Salt and black pepper

**Yield: 6 servings**

## FOR BOTH VERSIONS

**Optional:** Press the tofu for 20 minutes. Pressing extra-firm or super-firm tofu doesn't make much of a difference unless it seems very wet when it comes out of the package. If you choose to press your tofu, wrap the block of tofu in several paper towels or a clean kitchen towel and place on a plate. Place another plate on top of the tofu and weigh down the top plate. Cans or bags of beans or rice work well for this or a heavy skillet. This tower may start to topple as the tofu loses liquid, so don't use anything breakable, like glass jars, as a weight.

Cut the tofu block into bite-size cubes. You can do this however you want, but one way is to stand it on end and cut it vertically in half. Lay it down and cut into fourths, turn it 90 degrees, and then cut into fourths again.

**For the Crispy Panfried Tofu:** Line a large plate with a clean paper towel and set to the side.

Heat a large skillet over medium-high heat; cast-iron works best, but nonstick works, too. Add 1 tablespoon (15 ml) of peanut oil and let it heat up. Add half of the tofu cubes, spreading them out so they aren't touching; if your pan is on the smaller side, you may need to do this in three batches instead of two. If you have a splatter screen for your pan, this would be a great time to use it. If not, just be careful that you don't get splattered by the oil as it starts to pop. Cook the tofu 4 to 5 minutes on one side; do NOT move it during this time. It should flip easily when it's ready. If it's sticking when you try to flip it, let it cook another minute. You may use kitchen tongs, but a thin flat spatula may help if you find they are sticking. Flip all the pieces over carefully and cook for another 3 to 4 minutes. You may need to adjust the heat as you go; if your pan starts to get too hot, turn it down to medium. Flip the cubes one more time and cook for another 3 to 4 minutes. Turn the tofu cubes out onto the paper towel–lined plate in one even layer to drain any excess oil. Immediately sprinkle generously with salt and pepper.

Add the remaining tablespoon (15 ml) of peanut oil to the skillet and repeat with the remaining tofu cubes.

Three crispy sides is perfect, but you can certainly do all sides if you have the patience.

You can also just shake the pan each time instead of meticulously turning each one, but just know that some sides may get more done than others.

If you can resist eating them all straight from the plate, your tofu cubes are now ready to be used in a variety of dishes.

**For the Chewy Oven-Baked Tofu:** Place the tofu cubes into a shallow container or bowl. Whisk together the remaining ingredients, except salt and pepper. Pour the marinade over the tofu and toss well to ensure all tofu cubes are covered. Refrigerate for 15 to 20 minutes, tossing again after 10 minutes.

Meanwhile, preheat the oven to 375°F (190°C, or gas mark 5). Line a rimmed baking sheet with parchment paper.

Remove the tofu from the marinade. Place it in a single layer on the prepared baking sheet. Bake for 20 to 30 minutes, flipping every 10 minutes until golden brown, crispy on the edges, and chewy in the center.

Immediately sprinkle with salt and pepper while they're still hot.

# Soft White Buns

Plain. White. Buns. You honestly can't go wrong serving any of the burgers in this book on these buns.

1 cup (235 ml) plain soymilk or milk
    of choice
½ cup (120 ml) water
¼ cup (56 g) butter
4½ cups (563 g) all-purpose flour,
    divided
¼ ounce (7 g) quick-rise yeast
2 tablespoons (25 g) sugar
1½ teaspoons salt
2 eggs or equivalent (see Tip)

**Yield: 8 buns**

Line 2 baking sheets with parchment or a silicone baking mat.

In a saucepan or a microwave-safe bowl, combine the soymilk, water, and butter, and heat just until the butter is melted. (In the microwave, it takes about 1 minute.) Set aside.

In a large bowl, combine half of the flour and the yeast, sugar, and salt.

Add the soymilk mixture to the flour and mix well, then add the eggs or egg replacer.

After well incorporated, mix in the remaining flour, ½ cup (62 g) at a time.

Once all of the flour has been added, and the dough begins to form into a large mass, turn it out onto a floured surface and knead for 5 to 8 minutes, until smooth and elastic.

Divide into 8 equal pieces. Roll each piece into a smooth ball. Place on the baking sheets, 4 per sheet, and press down to flatten a little (like a disc, instead of a ball). Cover loosely and let rise for 1 hour.

Preheat the oven to 400°F (200°C, or gas mark 6).

Bake for 12 to 14 minutes, or until golden on top.

Let cool for 5 minutes on the pans before transferring to racks to cool completely.

> **Tip:** Make these buns with flax eggs (2 tablespoons [14 g] ground flaxseeds mixed with 6 tablespoons [90 ml] water), tofu eggs (½ cup [120 ml] blended silken tofu), or Ener-G (1 tablespoon [8 g] whisked with ¼ cup [60 ml] warm water until frothy). The best buns are with the Ener-G. The others taste fine, but won't puff up as much.

# 50/50 Flatbread

These easy flatbreads make a great stand-in for naan or pitas, and work well as a transportation device to get some of those yummy Middle Eastern–influenced burgers directly into your mouth. For another variation, add garlic and different herbs to dress up these little flatbreads.

Combine the flours and salt in a large bowl. Slowly add the water.

Mix with your hands until you get a nice big dough ball. Knead for a few minutes.

Divide into 16 equal pieces. Press each piece flat (about the size of a small pancake).

Using a dry, nonstick pan, cook each piece, one at a time, over high heat for 1½ to 2 minutes on each side.

If you have a gas stove, turn on an extra burner. After cooking in the pan, using tongs, place the flatbread on an open flame set to low for a few seconds. It will puff up and deflate quickly. Repeat on the other side.

Stack on a plate, under a dish towel to keep warm, until all the breads are done.

1½ cups (180 g) whole wheat flour
1½ cups (188 g) all-purpose flour
1 tablespoon (18 g) sea salt
1¼ cups (295 ml) water

**Yield: 16 flatbreads**

# Rustica Buns

Okay, so the name is a little goofy. But these buns really are rustic looking … and tasting. Enjoy these buns with all sorts of burgers, even on their own with melted butter, but you really have to try them with the Couscous Pantry Burgers on page 85.

In a mixing bowl, combine the chickpea flour, 1½ cups (188 g) all-purpose flour, yeast, baking powder, baking soda, and salt.

Add the tomatoes, garlic, and olive oil, and stir to combine.

Add the ½ cup (120 ml) water and knead well. Add more water, if needed, 1 tablespoon (15 ml) at a time, until a smooth, firm dough ball is formed. Knead for a few minutes, until uniform.

Divide into 4 equal pieces. Form each piece into a ball and then flatten slightly. Pat a bit of all-purpose flour onto each bun to coat. Place on an oiled baking sheet. Cover loosely and let rise for 1 hour.

Preheat the oven to 350°F (180°C, or gas mark 4).

Bake for 10 to 12 minutes, or until you see cracks forming on the tops.

½ cup (60 g) chickpea flour
1½ cups (188 g) all-purpose flour, plus more for coating
¼ ounce (7 g) quick-rise yeast
½ teaspoon baking powder
½ teaspoon baking soda
¼ teaspoon salt
¼ cup (28 g) finely chopped sun-dried tomato pieces
2 cloves garlic, minced
2 tablespoons (28 ml) extra-virgin olive oil
½ cup (120 ml) water, plus more if needed

**Yield: 4 buns**

# Cheesy Biscuits

Fluffy cheesy biscuits that taste great as a stand-in for a bun on any of the breakfast burgers in chapter 1. Depending on the type of milk used, this recipe can be made soy- or nut-free.

1 cup (235 ml) unsweetened soy or almond milk
2 tablespoons (30 ml) lemon juice
2¼ cups (281 g) all-purpose flour
¼ cup (30 g) nutritional yeast
2 tablespoons (25 g) sugar
2 teaspoons baking powder
1 teaspoon baking soda
1½ teaspoons salt
¼ cup (60 ml) refined coconut oil, chilled until solid
½ cup (50 g) finely chopped chives (optional)

**Yield: 8 biscuits**

Preheat oven to 450°F (230°C, or gas mark 8). Line a baking sheet with parchment or a silicone baking mat.

Combine the soymilk and lemon juice in a small bowl. It will curdle and become like buttermilk.

In a large mixing bowl, combine the flour, nutritional yeast, sugar, baking powder, baking soda, and salt.

Using a pastry cutter or your fingertips, work chilled coconut oil into the flour mixture until it resembles fine crumbs.

Create a well in the center and add the buttermilk mixture. Mix gently and sprinkle in the chives, if using. Gently knead until it comes together, taking care not to overwork the dough.

Turn the dough out onto a well-floured surface and form the dough into a rectangle about ¾ inch (2 cm) thick. Using a cookie cutter, or an inverted pint glass, cut the dough into rounds. Gently reform the dough as needed to get 8 biscuits.

Arrange in a single layer on the baking sheet, with the biscuits slightly touching each other, and bake for 12 to 15 minutes, or until lightly browned.

Let rest for 5 minutes before serving.

# Sweet Potato Buns

These soft and slightly sweet buns take potato rolls to a whole new level and are a reminder of why we make our own bread. The rolls work well on almost any burger.

Bring a pot of lightly salted water to a boil.

Peel and cut the sweet potato into chunks and boil until mushy. Meanwhile, stir the yeast and sugar into the warm water. Let sit for 10 minutes, or until doubled in size.

Drain the potatoes. Return to the pot, and mash.

Add the ¼ cup (56 g) butter, soymilk, and agave nectar. Mash until very, very smooth, with as few lumps as possible.

In a separate, large mixing bowl, combine the 4 cups (500 g) flour and salt. Add the yeast mixture to the flour and salt and stir to combine. Add the potato mixture and knead for 8 to 10 minutes, adding more flour if the dough is too sticky.

Knead right in the bowl until a soft, elastic dough ball forms.

Cover loosely with a dish towel, and let rise for 1 hour.

Preheat the oven to 350°F (180°C, or gas mark 4). Line 2 baking sheets with parchment or a silicone baking mat.

Punch down the dough and knead for about 2 minutes. Add a little more flour if the dough is too sticky.

Divide into 12 equal pieces, roll into balls, and flatten slightly. Place 6 on each baking sheet.

Bake for 12 to 15 minutes.

Remove from the oven, brush with extra melted butter, and bake for 5 minutes longer, or until golden brown on top.

1 large sweet potato or yam
½ ounce (14 g) active dry yeast
2 teaspoons sugar
½ cup (120 ml) warm water
¼ cup (56 g) butter, melted, plus more
    for brushing
1 cup (235 ml) soymilk
2 tablespoons (42 g) agave nectar
4 cups (500 g) all-purpose flour, plus
    more if needed
1 teaspoon salt

**Yield: 12 buns**

# Index